MENTAL

MENTAL

BAD BEHAVIOUR, UGLY TRUTHS
& THE BEAUTIFUL GAME

JERMAINE PENNANT

with JOHN CROSS

JOHN BLAKE

Published by John Blake Publishing,
an imprint of Kings Road Publishing
2.25, The Plaza,
535 Kings Road,
Chelsea Harbour
London, SW10 0SZ

www.johnblakebooks.com

www.facebook.com/johnblakebooks 🖪
twitter.com/jblakebooks 🗨

This edition published in 2018

ISBN: 978 1 78606 961 0

British Library Cataloguing-in-Publication Data:

A catalogue record for this book is available from the British Library.

Design by www.envydesign.co.uk

Printed and bound in Great Britain by Clays Ltd, Elcograf S.p.A.

1 3 5 7 9 10 8 6 4 2

Papers used by John Blake Publishing are natural, recyclable products made from
wood grown in sustainable forests. The manufacturing processes conform to the
environmental regulations of the country of origin.

Every attempt has been made to contact the relevant copyright-holders, but some
were unobtainable. We would be grateful if the appropriate people could contact us.

John Blake Publishing is an imprint of Bonnier Publishing
www.bonnierpublishing.com

CONTENTS

CHAPTER 1

GROWING UP FAST

If you have a difficult upbringing, then it's bound to affect you in your adult life. I just didn't realise at the time just how much it would affect me.

I grew up on a tough estate in Nottingham, the Meadows. It wasn't so much working-class. More what people might call lower-class. That's the simple truth. I think that if I'd had a different upbringing, my mum and dad always on the scene, then I would have played for England, would have had a bigger career, for sure. I've had a good career. I'm not unhappy. But I could have done more. I know that; I'm the first to admit it.

But a difficult childhood affects you when you grow up. Even now, it affects me. Certain choices I make. I went and saw someone, a psychologist; had six or seven sessions, telling them my story: why I made mistakes, why I would push people away, not let people get close to me. And the main reason was my childhood. Didn't have a mother figure; my father was disruptive.

Whenever people get close, I tend to get scared, don't want to be let down again, so I push them away. Most kids have someone to put their arm round you when needed. I never had that. That's something that has always affected me and probably always will.

My mum, Debbie, left home. I didn't see her for years. She was told by her mum – my grandmother – to have nothing to do with her 'brown baby', and I was even told that she had died, only to discover later that she hadn't at all.

I watched my dad selling drugs, turning our house into a drugs den, becoming a heroin addict, leaving shotgun cartridges around the place, having the front door kicked in by police and ending up in prison. He was a gangster.

I know what people say about me. 'Here comes trouble, he's a troubled guy and he *is* trouble.' It's been the story of my career. But I want people to understand some of the reasons.

* * *

The Meadows was a council estate. We moved from house to house. My dad had several partners, and would go from one woman to another. We would move in with them, and vice versa, then they'd split up and I'd see a lot of different women come and go. At the time, I had stepmums, a handful of them, and not having my real mum as well had an impact.

My mum had separated from my dad, Gary, when I was a little kid, maybe about three. My dad would have me on the weekends. He'd take me back home to my mum's. One weekend he went to take me back – drop-off time – and no one was there. Went back home. Came back the next day and for six months my dad couldn't get in touch with my mum. She disappeared overnight. My dad told me that he couldn't get hold of her.

GARY PENNANT: I had him at weekends, took him back to his mum and one Sunday night she wasn't there. There was no answer at the door, phoned her every hour and this went on for a week and nothing.

Then I thought, 'Right, I'll have to do something.' I went to social services, we got a flat in the Meadows. I was very young, not even twenty or twenty-one, and, to be honest, it was a steep learning curve.

It's a friendly neighbourhood. But we, as a crowd, were very naughty. In fact, we were pretty notorious. The Meadows was a nice place because no one dared come and cause any trouble. But we took all our troubles out of the Meadows. I used to think the Meadows was a nice place to grow up, even though a lot of people were into the criminal side of things; but actually, there was no trouble inside the Meadows because we wouldn't do bad stuff on our own doorstep.

I met a partner. She moved in with me eventually. Me and my partner had a new baby boy and we had a family bond there. Obviously, Jermaine was going to miss his real mum. I wouldn't know at that stage just how much it would affect him. Obviously, it *has* affected him. We haven't really spoken about it much between ourselves really.

Then, after my mum had gone missing, disappeared without a word, my dad saw her out of the blue in Nottingham city centre, and he couldn't believe his eyes. He shouted at her, chased her down, and she just ran off. He later found out that she'd moved on with her life, met someone else and got married. It was one side of the story.

However, as I got older, I saw her from time to time, but I didn't actually ask my mum what had really happened. She just told me that my dad and his family had threatened her and told her never to come near me again. She said she always wanted to get in contact but was too scared of my dad and the family.

One day, I asked my dad's mum, my grandmother Cynthia – she's got no issues, she's been great – what happened and she told me that she never had anything against my mum but said that my other grandmother, my mum's mother, had said to her, 'I don't want anything to do with this brown baby. My daughter has got enough to deal with. You lot keep it and deal with it.'

There is no reason for her to lie or for my dad to lie. My dad was only nineteen at the time and I couldn't see a nineteen-year-old taking on the burden of a child on his own. I had to believe that story; I believe it's true.

My grandmother said that she had no bad feelings. She said to me that if I wanted to pursue my mother then she'd be right behind me. My dad said the same thing and that, if I wanted to get in contact, then it was fine.

But from when I was three, I didn't see my mum until I was thirteen. Then we *had* to get in touch because I needed a passport to go to play in Paris for England schoolboys. To get that passport I had to get a signed birth certificate. I don't know how it was set up, how my dad got in touch, but we met up for the first time in years and she signed the document and got the passport. And it was hard to be in touch. It felt like seeing my mum almost for the first time, because I had been so young when she left that I couldn't really remember much. It all felt so weird.

But the craziest thing of all was that, for a while, as far as I knew, my mum had died. But, as I later found out, she didn't die at all. I was with my agent, Sky Andrew, in his office after I had signed for Arsenal and there was a phone call. Sky then came in the room and said, 'Jermaine, I've just had a call. I've got some bad news: your mum's died of cancer – throat cancer.'

I asked who it was who had called. He said it was a member of my family, they said they were so sorry. I was never close to my mother. But even if you're not close, you are still saddened. Losing your mum or dad is different from losing a cousin, say, or whatever. I didn't break down, but I was sad. But that's how I had to grow up. Growing up on my own. That's how I dealt with stuff and emotions. I've always been on my own.

After I got the call to say she had passed away and I told everyone at Arsenal that I had found out about it, they gave me a few days off and I didn't know really what to feel because I was never attached.

They were very good, gave me some compassionate leave. They wanted to send some flowers, but I didn't know where to say they should send them – or where to send anything myself – because I had no address.

Then it just came out that she didn't pass away. I can't remember exactly what happened, who got in touch to say she was alive after all. To me, it wasn't a happy or sad moment. It was a blank. I just thought, 'Oh, she's alive, OK.' It felt blank. It was just so typical of my upbringing.

I was growing older and she's got two sons who are my stepbrothers, and they got in contact via social media. I responded and some of the family on my mum's side got in touch when I was doing well, moving up and into my twenties.

Then, in my early twenties, my mum and I started to speak a bit more, trying to be in touch regularly, sending a few texts – and it was fine for a while. Then it just kind of faded and drifted away.

Now, at the time of writing this, I've not spoken to her for four or five years. It's always been my dad and his mum – my grandmother – who have been on the scene, even though I've had my ups and downs with my dad.

My mother always tries to make amends, tries to speak, but I've never had that connection that most children have with their parents.

It came out in the press that my mum had died and I might have said in an interview or the press that she had passed away at a young age. That then became written and accepted. It gets repeated from time to time. But it wasn't like that and she's still alive to this day.

* * *

To be honest, I grew up on my own. My dad tried to do his best for me; without him I wouldn't have had a career. He played semi-pro for Ilkeston Town. At that time, it was big because he was always in the local paper. He was a left-footed central midfielder. I don't think he had my pace, but definitely had the skill, control, vision and all that. Looking back, I reckon he probably did his best bringing me up on his own. It wasn't easy.

I remember every single bit of detail about growing up so clearly. I've only reconnected in the last five years with my dad. From age thirteen or fourteen to my twenties, I cut ties with him because I realised I was in the public eye, being at Arsenal, being in the papers, and people were recognising me. It made me feel as if I were somebody, but the downside of that was that, when I was at Arsenal and Liverpool, I was always nervous when people would get to their heights – that's when their past starts to come out. That's why I cut ties with my dad, because of what I grew up with, what I'd seen and what I'd turned into.

Even when I was at school, I knew my dad was selling drugs. It's your father, so you're not going to say anything and you probably don't want to think about it. But at twelve or thirteen, I knew what was going on. I didn't complain, though, because he was providing for the family. I didn't really go without; I had football boots; I had clothes when I needed clothes.

GARY PENNANT: He was about thirteen when I first started having my real drug problems. It was devastating on the family. I come from a good background, good family, and it was different for me and for the family.

I was still living in the Meadows at that stage. Everyone took their trouble away from the Meadows. The older generation was looking out for the younger ones. It was like a Robin Hood kind of thing. You had the older ones doing all the drugs, gangs and guns. But as my dad said, if there was a problem, it would be dealt with, wherever – but just not on our own doorstep. They would all get in their cars, go and deal with the problem, and it would never be on their own manor and you wouldn't be scared to go out or anything. There was only the one incident when I heard a commotion and came outside, and my dad and all the crew were there. They were having a shoot-up at my neighbour's windows. That was the only time I saw trouble.

You would get fights between gang members. I saw my dad have a fight outside Meadows Boys' Club. That was over football, pool cues, snooker cues; it was all going off. I was shit-scared. I was only about ten then. You would've feared for your life.

But it definitely toughens you up for life. You'd never experience that now and, if I did ever come across that environment, I wouldn't be fazed. I grew up through it. It makes you a stronger person, for sure.

It's definitely changed for youngsters now from what I went through. If you're a young kid growing up as a footballer now, in an academy, it's a different world. They get the best kit, best equipment, and it's as if they'd been born with silver spoons in their mouths. They are earning more money now and I'm not sure whether it's a good thing. They may be hungry, but I think it's a different hunger. My goal was to get out from where I came from, be the best I can, make something of my life. Now they just want to be like Cristiano Ronaldo; they want to be famous. You want to play in the first team, earn money, but I think they've got different goals and are striving for different things from me because I was trying to get things that I could never have.

* * *

My dad was always with different women. It wasn't until I was about nine that he met my stepmum, who has a son, Jaydon, whom I grew up with. From when I was eight to when I was sixteen, he met someone, settled down and had a child. But, all through that time, I knew he was selling drugs.

At first, he wasn't selling from home. It would be from the pub, the Three Bridges, which was a stone's throw from the house. It was incredibly close. Everyone met up there, it was brilliant. All the old people were there, the Meadows crew, the young kids and friends. It was like a proper meeting place. Everyone would meet there, talking football, and it was great.

Selling drugs there, seeing drugs there, was completely normal. And I reckon that if it hadn't been for football and my good friends looking out for me, I would have ended up doing the same. I love football and I always wanted to be a footballer, no matter what. I still wanted to be with my friends, still wanted to hang out and do stuff with them, but they always kept me at arm's length.

When they were going to do something, and if they thought it would jeopardise me or my football, they would always say, 'Look, you're not coming with us. We don't want you around.' I always wanted to be with my friends but I knew what it meant and I would just stay behind. They were great mates, always looked out for me. It was a tight group. I don't think I could ask for better mates.

But it was a tough upbringing. I saw so many things that you sometimes forget one incident to the next. But I witnessed a murder, even got questioned in connection with the murder – and that's something you never forget.

I was about fourteen. I was out with an older lot. We went to a party. We had a little Meadows crew. After it finished there was a gang from another area, St Ann's, hanging around.

When the party finished, one of our lot said, 'Just be careful – there's some of the St Ann's crew around.' They *were* hanging around, and it felt a bit dodgy. The group began to get bigger and bigger.

There were a few of us in Kentucky Fried Chicken – or KFC – and a few standing outside. And then, all of a sudden, they must have charged at us. They stabbed one of our friends in the shoulder, even though he didn't even realise he'd been stabbed until all the fighting had all finished.

They had knives, baseball bats and some guns. I don't honestly know if they were loaded with live ammunition or if they were firing blanks. But, as they ran past, they stabbed one and hit another with a baseball bat, and a few shots went off. They all ran off. Our gang chased them. I didn't see it, but one of the St Ann's gang got caught, they turned on him and he later died in hospital.

GARY PENNANT: When he was thirteen or fourteen, I remember telling him, 'I don't want you to get into trouble.' He came back one day with a CD. He'd stolen it. He was only twelve. I sat him down and I said to him, 'Jermaine, if you ever want anything, I will get it for you. And, if I can't, then I'll steal it for you!' But I told him I didn't want him to get into trouble because it would affect his life as well as his football. He was sensible.

I remember that he was hanging round with a group who were selling drugs at the time and I remember telling them that if they did anything illegal, they should make sure Jermaine went home. And they did.

I remember an incident when he was fourteen. It was with ten of the Meadows lads. They saw their rivals from another area. Apparently, a gun had been fired. They gave chase and the gang kicked a guy to death. Ten Meadows lads were on trial for murder. But there was only Jermaine and one of his mates who did not chase after them. They stood still and then went home. That whole incident could have changed his life. That choice he made to not go with his friends probably changed his life for the better.

He also listened and stayed out of trouble. That's why I always say parents have got a big say in how their children grow up. I think it's 80 per cent down to parenting.

A few people, including me, jumped over the counter in KFC. To me, at the time, it didn't really feel like a sliding-doors moment because I was just hanging out with my mates. The KFC thing was another gang thing. I was inside KFC, a rival gang came running past and they shot at a few people inside. They hit someone outside and they ran off straightaway. Everyone outside chased them away but I was inside KFC at the time. Someone died and that was when six of them got charged with murder.

My mate Christopher Joseph was with me. He was driving that night. When everyone dispersed, he drove and was looking for me. But I was still in Kentucky. I had jumped over the counter – and stayed hiding there! It was like a movie. I heard the shots and jumped for my life! Half an hour later, I found Christopher and he picked me up. Then, two days later, he was arrested. Then the police came for me, took me to the station, questioned me. You don't really think about it at the time but they're questioning you about a murder.

I was scared shitless. I was only about fourteen or fifteen at the time. I was scared about saying the wrong thing, worried about getting my friend in trouble. I just told them what I knew and what I could tell them wouldn't get him into trouble. I was just hiding behind the counter in KFC, nicking some chicken wings!

MENTAL

Christopher had told the police that he was searching for me and maybe that was why they came for me. They were shocked when they knocked on my door. They were expecting someone in his late teens, early twenties. Then, my stepmum told them that I'd be back at 3.30 p.m., when I got in from school. They both looked at each other, completely puzzled. They told my stepmum, 'We're here to question Jermaine Pennant.' She replied, 'He's at school.' They were investigating a shooting, they were looking for suspects and were told one of them was still at school!

My stepmum told me, 'The police came for you, the CID.' I knew then it was big business and I could be in trouble.

To be honest, I don't actually know why they came for me. Maybe Chris was using me as an alibi, or perhaps I was on the CCTV jumping over the counter. I had been arrested when I was younger for nicking a CD, so it could be they had my details on file.

They were asking what happened, what car; I had to describe what he was wearing. I was really scared, because I knew that if I got charged with murder, I could be going to prison for a long, long time. But Christopher was acquitted. He was a really good guy. He was with the gang, but he didn't get himself into too much trouble.

All six of those who stood trial for murder were acquitted. There was no evidence to say who was involved or what happened because the witness evidence didn't stand up in court.

Don't get me wrong: a kid from the other gang died, and it was nothing to celebrate. But everyone I knew was clear.

It all stemmed from a gang war. Someone from the Meadows killed someone from St Ann's with a baseball bat after an argument. Ever since then there's been a rivalry, and that was where it all began.

My dad was part of that and I can't deny that I knew what he was doing. It even got to a stage where he was selling drugs from the house. The more money you made, the more comfortable he got, and he got a bit lazy. Doing it at the house was when things started going downhill. So not only was he *selling* it from the house, they were *doing* it there as well.

They were smoking heroin. I could smell it. I didn't have to see it. Being around that environment while growing up, you know what's what. You know what crack smells like. You know what marijuana smells like. You know what cigarettes smell like. The drugs smell a bit like cigarettes but give off a worse, different stench. Sometimes I would bring my friends over and they could smell it, too. It was upsetting and so embarrassing for me. I used to bring my girlfriend round and I was ashamed. It used to eat me up inside. So many times I wanted to express my feelings to my dad but I just didn't know how.

A couple of years later, I was about to get up for school and the house was raided. It was about 7 a.m. and I was still in bed. All I heard was banging. The door flew off, police were running upstairs and I was thinking, 'I haven't done anything!' That was my first thought. I thought they were after *me*!

A couple of days before the raid, my friends and I were messing about near a skip and we saw some Pogs, which were really popular at the time. They're those little things that you'd flip and play with. All the kids were into them. I saw them in a skip in a pile of magazines. I don't know if they were faulty or what, but they'd been thrown away. I took an absolute load of them and I put them all in my cupboard. It looked like a supermarket display for Pogs. I remember the police raid. They ran up the stairs, looked in, shuffled around, and I was thinking, 'Oh, no, they've come for me!' Then they just left my room and took my dad away. Then I realised what it was all about. I've never been so afraid, so scared and so terrified of what my dad would say.

I had boxfuls of these things. I remember taking them to school. It was around a quid to buy a packet over the counter, but I was selling a box with about twenty packs inside for £2.50. I had a good friend at the time and we were selling them together. I was making loads of money!

My friend came to me and told me that the school had got wind of what was going on. 'Have you got any Pogs?' They were all in my backpack. My friend took them off me and hid them for me.

Then, an hour later, I was called in to see the headteacher. 'Can we check your bags, Jermaine? Are you selling anything?' I was all innocent-looking. 'No, not at all, Miss.' They looked in the bag. Nothing in there. I was so lucky not to be expelled! Obviously, the police weren't after the Pogs: they were after my dad.

My dad was arrested, so I stayed in the house with my stepbrother and stepmum. Because of the activity that went on at the pub, it was under surveillance. Cameras were in there and the police were watching it, which is why we got raided.

There was a warehouse across from the pub and apparently that was famous for what was going on there as well.

The day my dad got arrested I went to Meadows Boys, the youth club. There were older people there as well and I asked about what was going to happen to my dad. A lot of people got arrested that day. It was a big raid on a few houses – a big operation. Everyone was talking about it at the youth club. Someone said he could get six years and I remember then breaking down and crying. He was the only parental figure I had. I didn't have a mum. I had a stepmum, but she wasn't my mum. He was the only person. I looked up to him. I know he wasn't the greatest role model, but he was family; he is my dad. I know it wasn't great, but he couldn't get a job and was doing the best he could.

* * *

Dad didn't do that long in prison. He probably got about a year and did about six months. I remember that I went to visit him only once and he had a jumpsuit on with an orange bib, as if he was playing netball or something – that kind of bib. I remember getting him some chocolate. It was great to see him. When he came out he was very big because he'd been spending all his time in the gym. I just thought that would be over and he'd go back to normal life. But then he obviously got back into it. I think he tried to get on the straight and narrow, but started selling again. I was about thirteen or fourteen, and you put two and two together and you realise what's going on.

But this time it was worse. Dad started to sample it himself, he was trying heroin and then got addicted. He was known for being a drug dealer in the Meadows, started to take it, got hooked and became an addict. It was probably one of the worst sights I've ever seen. It really, really did tear me apart. I hated him for it.

It was a really bad point in my life; it was difficult. Growing up when he was addicted to heroin, I hated him and I never wanted to have anything to do with him.

I'll always remember one particular birthday. I think I was fourteen. I got a few cards from my grandma and a few family members. There was about £40 in there altogether and my dad said, 'Did you get any money? Have you got any money?' I told him I'd got some for my birthday. He just said, 'OK, give it to me and I'll give it you back.' I knew why he wanted it. I knew I wasn't going to get it back, because he was now addicted to this stuff. He'd not got a job and he was not even selling it any more because he was using it all.

It took over his whole life. 'Give me money.' How do you tell your dad no? So, basically, he took it off me. I remember crying. He told me to stop crying, stop being stupid, and he'd give it back to me. I've never seen the money since.

It was so bad seeing him coming home, seeing the way he was with all the people he would hang around with. He was on that stuff for ten years, and that's a long time to be taking it. Then he started taking it and trying to sell it again, and the only saving grace, I reckon, was when he got put in prison for two years for supplying again. He tried to sell some to an undercover police officer. I think I was about twenty when that happened.

I've got to admit that I got arrested as a kid. I was shoplifting a CD from HMV in Nottingham. It was a boy band – I can't remember which. I was walking out of the shop, the alarm went off and this big guy took me into the back of the store. They called my dad, and eventually he was sitting there while I was being questioned. But he was sitting there, reading his newspaper, not looking, just reading. They asked me, 'Why did you do it?' To be honest, I just said I couldn't afford it and I wanted the CD. That's how it was.

* * *

It was as I was starting to progress in my career that I began to lose contact with my dad. When I left Nottingham, that was when I distanced myself from him, and I didn't really want to be associated with him.

MENTAL

My grandmother would tell me about what he was up to. She said he needed help, that he looked like a skeleton, and I would be embarrassed to be seen in public with him or to bring him to football matches. That was what hurt, because I always wanted my dad there. When I was younger, he was my idol. He used to come to my games. Sometimes I didn't like it because he would tell me off if I wasn't doing the right thing in a match when all I wanted to do was enjoy it. I'd try to take four people on, score three goals, and he would be telling me off, trying to tear into me from the sidelines. I hated that. He would shout at me and tell me come inside, do this, do that. It was nerve-racking and could put me off my game.

But he stopped coming while he was taking another turn for the worse, and when it takes hold of you it's very hard to get out of it. When he went to jail for those two years, I prayed that it would change him. But the people he was friends with weren't great because they were on it as well; they were other addicts. His close friends were living different lives.

But two of his closest friends, Steven and Henry Warner, took him into a house and locked him in there for a few weeks to try to wean him off it. That cleaned him up. It was never going to be easy. Even in prison they gave him drugs to substitute for the heroin. He knew he had to do *something*. He's not a weak person, but once you try something, get addicted, it's hard. However, once he put his mind to it, I knew he could give up, for the sake of his family, for me, for Jaydon and the two sisters we've got, Rochelle and Lavelle. They are still in the Meadows; they still see my father there. They used to tell him he had to fix himself up. I remember my brother telling him, 'It's not right, fix yourself up, I don't want you round my daughter when you're like this.'

I was never tempted to try it. Maybe it was because I saw the destruction it caused. I despised that, I despised it – the drugs and the people my dad hung around with. I tried cigarettes – all the kids did – but I never enjoyed even them. I didn't like the smell of them. Maybe it's because I had smelled the drugs in our house. Mentally, it put me off. I never wanted to go down that path.

I tried marijuana once. Funnily enough, it was my dad who let me try it and I think he wanted to teach me a lesson. It was in the house; he had some friends round and he was having a few beers. He was smoking the stuff, playing some music, and it was fun to see them all socialising. I didn't see marijuana as a harmful drug. The effects weren't the same as heroin or crack in the way that they destroyed his life, making him steal money and tearing him apart.

Marijuana was like a social drug. Heroin is a banned substance and is very dangerous. I'm not condoning marijuana, because it's illegal. But it felt different. As I've said, my dad let me try it and within a few minutes I had smoked some, breathed it in, and remember throwing up everywhere. I was so sick. I remember looking round and they were all laughing. My dad was pissing himself laughing and his words were, 'That'll teach you a lesson.' It bloody did! I was twelve. Since then, I was never tempted.

But I knew and had seen things at such an early age that most adults will never see in their lives.

* * *

The area I grew up in was full of gangs. You'd often have gang warfare going on. There were different gangs: Meadows, St Ann's and Radford. Gangs had been rife since my dad had been young and it's been going on ever since. I think it's calmed down a bit – but it's still happening.

I remember one time being in the kitchen at home and there was a JD Sports bag. I opened it up, thinking, 'What's this?' I remember seeing a load of cartridges. It was only about four years later, when I was about fifteen or sixteen, that I realised what it was. They were shotgun cartridges. When I first realised, I thought, 'Shit! I was playing with shotgun cartridges.' They were my dad's. He was in a gang and he had them in the house.

I remember my friends coming over one time and, looking under his bed. I found a Desert Evil silver gun. It wasn't loaded but it was a heavy thing, looking like something straight out of a Clint Eastwood or John Wayne film.

I was showing it to my friends: 'Look at this, look at this.' They were astonished and yet to me it was kind of the norm.

I remember another time on my close when there was

loads of noise. I went outside to have a look and there was about fifty or sixty people hanging around near the pub opposite. I walked out all giddy and I remember seeing cars getting smashed. Across the road was my dad's closest mate at the time, Steven Warner. We used to call him Doc, short for Doctor. I remember seeing someone with a baseball bat smash the back window of his white Toyota MR2. He was leaning out of the window in his house, shouting, then all I heard was three shots aimed at him. I was standing outside and saw what was going on and I quickly reversed, walked back and disappeared back inside my house, then peered outside to see what went on.

It was gang warfare. The other gangs had come down to try to shoot up the Three Bridges pub. My dad had got a tipoff and stayed away. I thought they were going to kick Steven Warner's door down, drag him out and kill him. But, luckily, they just did what they did and left it.

At first I thought it was exciting. That was when I found the JD Sports bag. I remember seeing my dad with the bag across his shoulder going somewhere. I thought there would be retaliation. I was expecting it to go off.

I still idolised my dad at that point, and thought, 'My dad's a gangster!' He was well known, well respected, and I saw him get into a lot of fights. Much of it was to do with football. He was fighting on the pitch and was respected within his group.

As people get older, they all tend to calm down, but, with my dad, that was when he started to do the drugs as well.

MENTAL

He has realised he made mistakes, and has apologised for them – and for not being there for a big part of my life.

* * *

We did get back in touch – or, rather, he got in touch with me. I used to ignore it when I got phone calls and messages, because I didn't want to be associated with him. But my grandma would tell me that he was sounding better, doing better, looking better, and you knew when someone was back on the straight and narrow. He sounded better to me and he said, 'I've got a job now: I work on a building site.' He loves labouring; that's what he does. He would leave me a message saying, 'All right, son, I love you, going to bed now, got work in the morning.' To hear that was great. Finally, I had a parent now. Never had a mum, never had a phone call, never had that dominant figure of a father that men crave when they're growing up. That's affected me in my adult life. You can see it in the mistakes that I've made.

* * *

So it was great to finally get my relationship going with my father again. That happened later in my career, after I'd gone to Liverpool and then when I was at Stoke City.

He started coming to games again. He was born in Sheffield, is a Sheffield Wednesday fan, but is also a massive Liverpool fan. That was why I was a Liverpool fan, too, being at home watching football with him. Watching John Barnes videos from that era. I remember we played

Liverpool at Stoke. I had a box. He came to the game. I was on the bench. It was a great match. Liverpool won 5–2 after Suárez and Sturridge scored. All the Liverpool fans had their scarves and were singing 'You'll Never Walk Alone'. Then I looked up at my box and all I could see was Dad going, 'You'll *neh*-ver walk alone.' I was thinking, 'Are you sure? How about supporting your son?' He wasn't looking at the game: he was just looking at the Liverpool fans. I wanted to burst out laughing, seeing that. He was supposed to be there supporting his son!

GARY PENNANT: I was at Stoke and I couldn't help it! I'm a diehard Liverpool fan. It's a natural instinct!

I couldn't laugh because I was caught on camera while we were losing. He came to the FA Cup semifinal when I was with Stoke; other big games as well. We are fine now. He came to my wedding, was on the main table; that was an emotional day and that was good.

We're still a strange family, to be honest. We were tight but I think we fell apart when my grandma and granddad got divorced when I was about ten or eleven. That really had a huge impact on us. I remember we would go and meet up as a family, along with uncles and aunts, on a Sunday and we always used to talk about trying to get back together. Despite those big family conversations,

MENTAL

that's what really tore the family apart and broke us up. Eventually, I moved to London, my dad fell off the wagon and I don't think the family have ever really been repaired. I fell out with them over certain things and it's difficult to get it back.

CHAPTER 2

GETTING NOTICED

My earliest memory was kicking a ball. Even when I went to the local chippy, there I was, with the ball and a bag of chips, running home. I took a football everywhere. The number of times I got told off because my trainers or my trousers were battered! I could have ice skates on and I would still try to play football!

GARY PENNANT: His football started when he was maybe four, four-and-a-half. I took him on holiday to Bournemouth. I bought him a beach ball and the way that he kicked it and controlled it, I thought, 'Wow!' You know, if you've played football, when someone has got something. I went straight to the shop and bought a real football, found a patch of grass, and you could see that he was special.

MENTAL

I thought I must teach him, coach him, and he had the love of the game, so every day he wanted to play. If he wasn't out with a football then there was something wrong. He started from there and you could tell that if he kept out of trouble then he would make it.

My grandma would hate my going into the garden because Granddad loved gardening and he'd have all sorts of plants. The garden was immaculate. But after I'd been in there, my grandma would say I'd make it look like an earthquake. Half the plants would be on the floor, the lawn would be torn up, everything would be kicked out of place. Anything that was round, I would want to kick it. My dad would take me onto the local fields, teach me the basics and kick a ball to me.

It was when I was at primary school that I got noticed. At nine, my friend played for a team called Clifton All Whites. He told the coach that he had a friend who was good at football, and suggested he get me down for training. So I began to train with them regularly. I remember that the first time I went, they were all dressed in kit – shorts, boots, the proper stuff. I turned up in slacks, trainers and a T-shirt. I didn't have anything, certainly no suitable kit.

Anything I could get my hands on I would just wear to play football in. It was only later that I started appreciating nice trainers, nice kit. Then I would get it all scuffed and messy and my dad would give me a right good hiding.

The trial went well – but I was so hot and sweaty in those slacks! Even then, when I was nine, I was playing in a team for eleven-year-olds; they signed me up. You had to pay £2.50 as subs, and I was struggling, but, because I was the star of the team, I would pay when I could. I'd ask Dad for subs. Sometimes he had the money, sometimes not. Even when he had the £2.50, I would keep it!

I recall one big game against the local rivals. I think they were called Hucknall Harriers. Either they or we would win the league every year. They always used to have to come round to my house to get me because I had no transport. I remember that, before the game, there was a lot of banging on the door. Bang, bang, bang! 'Are you coming? We've got a game.' I just went back to sleep. 'Come on, it's Hucknall Harriers – we need you.' I got out of bed, played and we won 4–2. I remember it so well.

After that, I got spotted by Notts County. They had Junior Magpies. I got invited for a trial; I was about eleven. Your school would put you in for Nottinghamshire, the local City Boys. I got selected for the schools team and that was where I started to make my mark, because I was scoring four or five goals every game. I was a striker back then so I got compared to Andy Cole. He was from Nottingham and also played for the same City Boys team. People were saying that I was a better striker. So, if Andy reads this, then he'll know he's second best! I was in the local papers, the *Evening Post* and the football pull-out on a Sunday. The headlines were always something like 'Pennant bags four goals'.

GARY PENNANT: I knew all the pitfalls, because I had played semi-pro football. I played for a semi-pro team called Hucknall Town. You see, most black parents don't know about football. Our parents couldn't guide us in football. It was always a case of learn your lesson, be good at school and football was just a game to play with your friends. It wasn't something to strive for.

He just improved and improved. I think he was nine, played for the school team in a final at Nottingham Forest's ground. He just stood out and from that day on a few clubs came in and asked me, 'Who is he with? Has he signed for anyone?' At that moment, he wasn't with anyone. The first team to come in for him was Notts County and we just took it from there.

He was fourteen. I took him out of school a year early because he had so much talent. He went into digs with Notts County so he could concentrate on his football full time.

There were a lot of scouts back then. When I later signed for Arsenal after my stint with Notts County, one of the scouts said, 'We've been watching you since you were twelve.' They even had my marks and progression. You'd get A for skill, different marks for team work and goalscoring. They showed me the stats.

Someone told me that Manchester United were watching me when I was thirteen and invited me to go down for a trial. I can't really remember why but I didn't go. I don't think I was that interested.

I think the school sent the best players to City Boys for trials rather than leave them to be spotted by a scout.

I remember once when we were at City Boys, Jermaine Jenas and I didn't turn up for training one day. The manager tried to make an example of us at a subsequent match and put us both on the bench. We were losing 5–2 at half-time. They brought us on for the second half and we won 7–5. That taught them a lesson!

Jermaine and I knew each other well. We played for the same teams from around nine or ten. We never really hung out properly because we weren't from the same area. But we were both from Nottingham, both of us had success and we always crossed paths.

GARY PENNANT: From when he was nine, clubs wanted him. Everton, Villa, Arsenal – all came in for him. They spoke to me at the Forest ground. I wanted him to stay with me and I was hoping Forest would come in, but it was County who came in.

When I was at Notts County, I just shot through the ranks. I was never great at school. My punctuality was never perfect – and that's putting it mildly! When I was fourteen or fifteen, Notts County told the school they wanted to take me out for a whole year and the school thought it would be better for me. They got it through by saying it was a year's work experience. I was basically unofficially on the Youth Training Scheme (YTS) at fifteen when you weren't supposed to be on the YTS until you were eighteen. Yet there I was at fifteen playing with eighteen and nineteen-year-olds. Because I was so young, I couldn't get an official wage. The YTS wage was £48.50, but I had to go into the office, get a brown envelope and they would have to give it to me in cash. The YTS participants would have to do one day's college a week and I'd have to go and do that with them. It was business studies – that's always the easiest option.

I was living in the digs provided for the other YTS kids. They were opposite Nottingham Forest's ground, about five minutes from the Meadows. They put me in digs because they knew my background, what sort of people I was associating with, and they didn't want me going off the straight and narrow. There was nothing worse than investing in someone and seeing them mess it all up.

When I moved into the digs at Notts County, I missed my friends and my life. It was structured. You had to be in by 8 p.m. I was two minutes from home, but couldn't go back, and yet others were from all over. Half an hour, or whatever, from, say, Derby or Mansfield.

I got into trouble a few times. I realise, looking back, that I did get special treatment because Notts County knew what they had on their hands. I was at Forest before that but Forest was an upper-class club at the time. Notts County was a family club. The Forest kids all wore Puma Kings, Nikes or whatever. I had Gary Lineker Quasar boots. Their boots were all spick and span; my boots had last week's pitch all over them. I didn't fit in at Forest. The structure wasn't right and I went to Notts County. I remember someone saying that the biggest mistake Forest made was letting me go.

A man called John Gaunt owned the digs. He was a mean guy, a big guy, and he was good for me. It was a good experience for me, good to be around football, and it got me out of my life in the Meadows.

My first youth coach gave me his Uhlsport boots. No matter what conditions, how hard the pitch was, I'd be in studs and not moulds. You could hear me running down the pitch sounding like a horse, like hooves crashing down on the ground. The boots made such a racket!

Gary Brazil, one of the youth coaches, was great for me. You can feel it when someone looks out for you. He would put his arm round me, look out for me. Sam Allardyce was the manager at the time. I remember at fourteen training with the first team in a five-a-side game. Now it's unheard of. You'd never see academy players with the senior players. It just doesn't happen now. I took on one or two players and I scored.

I remember Sam Allardyce on the sidelines. You know how he is with his big head, his red face, leaning backwards to get his voice right from the gut. He would shout, 'Fuck! Fucking hell! He's only fourteen! Don't let him do that to you! You're a disgrace!'

I do remember Allardyce but we didn't really talk that much, to be honest. It was funny because I was fifteen years of age. I was put in the squad and got told to travel. That was massive for me at the time – just incredible. I remember I went from home, and there I was in my tracksuit, riding my bike to the ground to get the coach with the first team. I was on my bike pedalling, pedalling, pedalling. That's crazy! Then I put my bike in the changing room. Can you imagine that now? I sat there, waited for about half an hour and I'm thinking, 'Where *is* everyone?' Then someone came in and said, 'What are you doing?' I said I was waiting to get on the coach for the game. 'No, they left an hour ago!' I had bloody missed the bus! I'd got the time mixed up. That's me through and through. I'm still like that now and it's never changed even though I'm in my thirties. I was thinking, 'Sam's going to kill me.' But, for some reason, he seemed to accept my excuse and I didn't get into trouble. But, from that day on, I trained more and more with the first team. Then I made my debut with them in the FA Cup aged just fifteen and however many days, and became the youngest player in the competition. It was against Sheffield United, away.

Sam was scary but he was also funny. He didn't really shout at me, because I was only fifteen. A fifteen-year-old training with men was so different. I used to skip past players and score goals, and, as I said, he would go nuts at them. I used to feel bad, because I was only a kid and yet they were getting shit from their gaffer and I thought they'd be after me. I thought I'd have to stop doing that and I got scared because I got a few kicks.

Ian Hendon was a defender at the time and he gave me a few whacks. Alex Dyer was a player there at the time, too, and he was really good to me, would look out for me. They were actually a good bunch. If I'd stayed there, then, to be honest, I could have made a bigger impact.

I played in a cup game and got someone sent off. I almost scored as well. I remember the YTS lads all watching, all buzzing because I was so young. I went through. They were all on the touchline and they were saying, 'Don't score, don't score.' It was a Christmas Night out that night; they couldn't finish until the game had finished because they had to clean the dressing room and, if I scored, it would go into extra time, meaning an extra half an hour, and it would mean they couldn't go out! I didn't score. We lost 2–1. The game was finished and they were saying, 'Jermaine, so glad you didn't score!'

MENTAL

That was my first senior game in one of the cups, the Johnstone's Paint. As we've seen, I was fifteen when I made my debut in the FA Cup away at Sheffield United.

It didn't faze me, even though I was a boy playing against men. When I came on, the fans gave me such a cheer. It was a great moment and one I will always remember.

I remember being in the Youth Cup, playing against Joleon Lescott. Whenever I see him now he says, 'I made you.' I tore him to bits! I was turning him inside out, had a great game and he reckons that was when I came of age.

There was another game, playing against seventeen- or eighteen-years-olds in the FA Youth Cup, and this other defender was giving me so much stick. One of my teammates told me, 'Just tell him how old you are.' I was fifteen. It killed him!

I played for England schoolboys. I went to Lilleshall for a trial. It just didn't work out for me. When I went there, I was late – the story of my life. I didn't have a car, no transport, so my dad's friend Henry Warner gave me a lift. He dropped me off at Lilleshall. 'Sorry, I'm late,' I said – and I could see them all saying, 'Oh, he's one of them!'

They were all from big clubs. Jermain Defoe, Jay Bothroyd from Arsenal. They were all in club tracksuits and there I was in, last year's old kit. I had to go out and buy something from a warehouse shop – a makeshift Notts County strip. The shorts were wrong, but I wanted to be a part of what they were. I bought an England strip, with the grey shirt and I got a Liverpool kit. I didn't play for Liverpool then, and I could see them all going, 'What's he doing?' On the back it had number nine, Fowler! I looked so out of place; it looked ridiculous.

I enjoyed the training, but I remember one session sleeping in, missing breakfast. I felt so hungry and I remember saying to Jermaine Jenas, 'I need a Mars bar. I can't run any more.' When we were finishing the session, they told us to get the balls in. Now, I've always been a bubbly character, a bit lively, sometimes a bit lairy – not disrespectful or rude, just a bit of a character. So, when I went to get the balls in, I booted one of them and watched in horror as it crashed down onto the back of the coach's head!

Each day at training they give you a mark: A, B or C. I think if you get a C you are out and, sure enough, that day I got a C for attitude.

I was disappointed. I thought Lilleshall was England. I didn't really realise that Lilleshall was like a school. I was thirteen, I think, and I still went on to play for England schoolboys. But it shows my naivety at the time that I was thinking Lilleshall was the official England set-up, when it was basically an academy! If it was a different environment, where it was strict; maybe it would have made a difference, who knows?

FRIEND AND FORMER CHARLTON DEFENDER, JON FORTUNE: When you think of the others in his position, like Beckham, Wright-Phillips or David Bentley, Pennant is so talented. Apart from Beckham, who is better? Jermaine is so talented and, to an extent, he hasn't made the most of his talent or his ability and, yes, he should have played for England, won a lot of caps and had a great career.

He has done really well, had a far better-than-average career, and therefore he's been a massive success.

But he has enjoyed life. He's such a warm character. He came to my dad's fiftieth birthday party. We had a great night. He ended up getting so emotional and we all had some tears because he's not used to all that and the family way of life. He loved it.

I played for England at schoolboys, and the under-fourteens, under-fifteens, under-sixteens and under-twenty-ones. I remember being eighteen, playing for the under-twenty-ones, playing with John Terry, Paul Robinson and Alan Smith. We had a good team. I remember being a menace to them all! They were good times.

I think my highlight was playing in the Victory Shield, and I can remember that, straight afterwards, it was the moment when I became aware of big clubs being interested, and I'm told it was the moment that made Arsenal decide they wanted me.

It was when I was with England that I was put out on the wing. They put me on the right. Up until then I had always been a striker. Arsenal watched me on the right in the Victory Shield. I always wonder what would have happened if I had stayed as a striker.

But Les Reed, one of the England coaches at the time, told me that I was better suited to playing wide and he put me on the wing. He just picked the team, put it down on paper and said I was on the right. I just wanted to play and, to be honest, I used to drift out to the right, anyway. He could see I was quick. He just wanted me to get down the line, put the ball over and get involved.

Once they put me on the right, my crossing started to let me down. I started to practise crossing, whipping the ball – I would work on it non-stop, always trying to whip it in. At sixteen, I can remember watching David Beckham. He could cross a ball so well. He was amazing, but I'm sure Beckham would say that he worked on it a lot as well. He was my inspiration to start whipping the ball. It got better and better and eventually I mastered it myself, now it's probably the strongest part of my game.

Up until then I would try to get to the by-line, try to dink it in and put it across. But I really worked on my game.

MENTAL

I was making great progress at Notts County, playing with the first team in training, making my mark with England and it was all coming together.

But then, as with most things in my life, just when I thought it was going well, I went and made the biggest mistake of my career. To this day, I look back and regret it, and will always wonder what would have happened if I hadn't made that mistake. And that mistake was everything to do with signing for Arsenal.

CHAPTER 3

FROM BACK PAGE TO FRONT

My transfer from Notts County to Arsenal in 1999 made headline news. Sadly, the transfer was on the front pages rather than the back because it was such a scandal. That is just so typical of my career really.

But it has since been news all over again because it involved the agent Mark Curtis and the then Notts County manager Sam Allardyce who became embroiled in a newspaper sting that led to his losing his job as England manager.

Allardyce was filmed by undercover reporters giving advice on how to get round the Football Association's rules on third-party ownership. Back in 1999, it was Curtis who was taped offering my dad money to set up a transfer, which is also against FA rules.

So my transfer was big news – the front-page splash on the *Sunday People* – because it was unheard of for a schoolboy to move from one club to another for £2 million. It was a record at the time, but that was only half the story. The real story was full of scandal and bungs, and it involved big names.

I was signed to another agent, Sky Andrew. From those early days, he has become a major influence in my life, a father figure, and we're very close. My auntie Diane called Sky and asked him if he would be interested in looking after me; he came to my house in Nottingham for a meeting and the rest is history.

I first met Sky when I was a kid. He couldn't find where we lived, so he drove to the train station in Nottingham, let me know when he was there and then I jogged all the way there. I met him in the car and took him to my house. He had an old, sky-blue Mercedes SL at the time. And he was shitting himself! He thought as soon as he parked outside my house that his wheels would get taken. He kept on looking out of the window.

AGENT, SKY ANDREW: I'd heard he was a good player and his auntie Diane contacted me and told me there were a lot of agents around. She'd heard of me and wanted me to come and meet the family.

I went to Nottingham. I couldn't find the house, so I parked in Nottingham station. Jermaine literally ran to the station and I saw this little kid with bandy legs bounding towards me. It was him. He got in the car, we drove back to his house in the Meadows and had the meeting with his family

He said to me, 'I live in the Meadows.' I didn't think much of it. Then I saw it and said, 'Are they gonna nick my wheels?' He promised the car would be all right. We had the meeting and we got on really well. He was a right cheeky little kid. I wanted to clip him round the ear because he was so cheeky.

In those days I'd speak to his aunt Diane most of the time and his dad was all right. We'd speak now and again but it was mainly his aunt.

Sky spoke to my dad and my stepmum. My dad was always unsure on Sky. He's never really been a fan. They've not really seen eye to eye. But he can't knock him, because he eventually got me to Liverpool, and that was always my dad's dream.

It was my auntie who made the introduction to Sky and my dad fell out with her over it. He thought we could put everything together on a transfer and we didn't need an agent. When he found out that my aunt had been in touch with Sky, that was when he went mad with her!

But I liked him and I've been very loyal to him. I stayed with him, but the move from Notts County was all done behind his back, without my knowing much about it either. I think the first Sky knew about it was when a journalist called Shaun Custis called him and asked if he had a comment about my joining Arsenal. To be honest, I was just a young kid and I didn't know what was going on.

I remember I was in the digs when it all started. Mark Curtis must have done a deal with my dad, and also done a deal with Notts County, and Notts County also did a deal with Arsenal. Notts County gave the go-ahead. I was in the digs watching TV with the rest of the lads. John Gaunt came down, came in the room and said, 'J, I've got to talk to you. You've got to go. You're going to Arsenal.' I couldn't believe it. What was he going on about? No planning, no say in the matter, I was being told, 'You're going there.' Sky had told me and my dad that the best thing for me was to stay and finish my schooling, then look at the situation again in the summer.

SKY ANDREW: They stuck him in the first team at Notts County. People were enquiring about him, his reputation was growing and most teams knew about him. They were contacting Notts County and his dad would ask me, 'What do you think?' I was telling them to stay until the end of the season, because that was the end of the school year, to do his GCSEs. Get schooling out of the way, no upheaval.

Then it got a bit tasty when we started hearing various clubs were interested. I was telling his aunt that he should stay put, but the strained relationship between her and Jermaine's dad was becoming a problem. Neither me nor Jermaine's aunt knew how much contact there had been between third parties and his dad. But it came to a head and he moved to Arsenal.

I spoke to Sam Allardyce and the Notts County chairman and said to both of them that he was going to stay until the end of the season.

I was round my girlfriend's house and a journalist called me and said, 'What comments have you got on your client joining Arsenal?' I thought that was strange. I tried calling Jermaine and then his dad and couldn't get hold of either of them. I rang the Notts County chairman and couldn't get hold of him, either.

I couldn't believe it. I told them to stay put, be patient and wait until the end of the season. I was concerned about the upheaval from his schooling. He was a type of kid that needed to prepare properly for any move. Let's say he'd had a tough upbringing and needed a lot of guidance. Plus, his family were Liverpool supporters and had expressed the desire for him to play for them. If they waited, then Jermaine could finish school and explore all options properly. He was the most sought-after talent in the country at that time. Then suddenly you've got headlines: '£2m teenager signs for Arsenal'.

For me, it was weird because people were calling me saying, 'Great deal. . .' blah, blah. Well, I didn't do it. Everybody knew he was signed to me but for people to get round me they had to go to his dad and try to get something done. Shame, really, because, although he went to a great club with fantastic individuals like Liam Brady, the whole thing affected Jermaine like a rabbit caught in headlights. I realised something massively underhand had gone on but didn't know what.

At the time when the journalist called me I didn't know who was involved. I was obviously very interested in who was involved in the deal. I did some digging and found out that another agent had gone to see Jermaine's dad and a deal had been done. I was really frustrated for Jermaine, because I had been very careful in gradually helping him develop and get ready for the future.

My dad didn't let me ring anyone, just took me to the train station and we went to London to do the deal. Maybe I should have suspected something when my dad was behaving as he was. It didn't seem quite right.

Mark Curtis offered my dad money, a house and a job if I signed for Tottenham. But, then, my dad didn't want me to sign for Spurs at the time because he thought the manager at the time, George Graham, was a 'cunt'. They were his exact words. 'He's a cunt, so I don't want my son to sign for him.' That's what he said. I never got told about this; I was never in the loop.

The reason why my dad was thinking about a move, was that I was losing my way a bit. I was missing training because I just wanted to hang out with my friends. Half of my childhood got taken away and that probably played a part in why my attitude towards certain things in football had changed. Although I started to miss training, I was well advanced: I was fourteen, training with seventeen-year-olds and began to get a bit carried away, complacent, and thought I could miss training.

I wanted to stay in Nottingham, but my dad began to think I needed to get away. He didn't fancy Tottenham, but Mark Curtis then mentioned Arsenal, because they had contacted Notts County. It was Notts County who then told my dad that Arsenal had made an approach, but they made it clear they wanted me to stay. They said it was better for my progression and development. Notts County had offered a contract for £500 a week, which was very good money for where I was at then. Very good money. But I think my dad must have been tapped up before then, because he kept telling me not to sign it. 'Don't accept it, don't accept it.'

Mark Curtis had heard about Arsenal's interest. He must have been tipped off about it. It's obvious that Curtis is close to Allardyce, as they've been a partnership for years. Then, the next minute, Mark Curtis had said to my dad that, if I signed for Arsenal, he would get £20,000 – £10,000 when I signed scholarship forms and another £10,000 when I signed as a pro. My dad was probably a bit naïve.

MENTAL

GARY PENNANT: I got a phone call from a guy called Mark Curtis. He came in, he said he wanted to meet me and talk about Jermaine. We met at the Royal Hotel in Nottingham. He told me Tottenham were interested in him and if he signs for them then they will give me a house, money and a job in London.

But at the time it was George Graham who was manager and, even if I wanted to then, I wouldn't let him go Tottenham. I didn't really like the club or him as a manager. He was too strict and I know how Jermaine is! He needs a bit of leeway.

Even then, I didn't want him to leave Nottingham, because he was only fifteen then. Not long afterwards, I got a call from Notts County asking me to go to a meeting with them and they said that Arsenal were interested in him. I was thinking that the transfer was between County and Arsenal.

Sam Allardyce said he shouldn't go and that he would be a small fish in a big pond at Arsenal and should stay at County. He definitely wanted him to stay. But I've heard subsequently that Sam and Mark Curtis work closely together.

I know my dad definitely got the first £10,000 of the £20,000 promised in the deal. He gave a bit to my stepmum at the time. Mark Curtis met my dad in a car park, gave him another £700 in an envelope, and that's the story he gave to the papers. I don't know how or where he gave my dad the first £10,000 – whether it was direct or to the newspaper – but, either way, my dad got £10,000 for the deal, for my signing for Arsenal. Mark Curtis acted for Arsenal because Sky Andrew was my agent. At that stage, at the age of fifteen, I had no idea how things worked, who got paid, what happened in transfers and so on. One minute I was training at Notts County and the next minute I was driving down to London with my dad and Mark Curtis. I think it was Mark who drove us down. After Sam, my dad spoke to Liam Brady, who was head of Arsenal's youth setup, and, once we signed, we spoke to Arsène Wenger.

GARY PENNANT: We decided to go down and meet Arsenal and Liam Brady, who was youth team coach at the time. I had a word with Liam, liked what he had to say. He was an excellent footballer in his day.

What swayed me was not just Liam Brady and Arsenal, an excellent team, and Arsène Wenger, an excellent manager, but that we had family in London at the time. His aunt lived there, he was close to his aunt and I wouldn't have let him go to London if he had nobody down there.

I spoke to him and he wanted to go. The next day I got a call from Sky Andrew, who was absolutely fuming. I thought it was between the two clubs.

MENTAL

Back in those days I wasn't clued up on transfers, but Sky Andrew heard who it was and who was involved and Sky knew about Mark Curtis and he told me that it was wrong. Now I know football and the ins and outs; I know it was wrong.

I felt angry that Curtis had pulled the wool over my eyes. Sky then told me he was taking Curtis to an FA tribunal. It got out in the press that there was some wrongdoing in that deal.

A newspaper rang me and asked if I would help them do a story. We fixed it up. I was wired up. I met Curtis and he did say those things again, that if he signed for Tottenham then he would promise me lots of things.

Now I know better, I'm not sure I would have done it.

He was fifteen-and-a-half back then; he knew how good he was for his age; he knew how much County valued him and was starting to miss training a bit. He wanted to play out with his friends a bit. He was missing out on being a normal fifteen-year-old. He was taking the piss a bit with County and I thought it was time for him to leave County and go to a better club. Sometimes, on a match day, he wouldn't turn up and they'd have to come to the house to pick him up. So I thought it was time to get him away from his mates.

The next day, after I'd signed, we came back on the train, and on the other side of the carriage was someone reading the paper. I looked and there was a picture of me in my England schoolboy kit on the front page. There I was, a kid from Meadows, on the front page involved in a scandal. As soon we were off the train, my dad bought the paper and ever since then I've been in the limelight.

I can't remember too much about Mark Curtis, apart from his being quite small, stocky and fat. I've not really seen him since then. I was too young to take it all in and strike up much of a relationship. I think my dad regrets what happened. But, and I know it wasn't great, I still achieved my dream and played for Liverpool, so I can't complain about that.

SKY ANDREW: Jermaine's dad called me one day and he was crying. I told him that I'd advised him to stay put. He said an agent had offered him money. Journalists were calling him and he was panicking.

In the meantime, he had done an agreement with a newspaper – like a sting – to expose Curtis in a car, in a motorway service station. His dad felt aggrieved that he had been conned in a way and that he was not going to get all of his money, so he did another story with another paper and got paid.

The papers were all over him at that time. I was

angry and I said that he'd gone behind my back. He was under pressure from so many people and it was such a big story at the time.

I don't know fully what went on. But it was a strange time.

What has happened since with Sam Allardyce losing his job as England manager did surprise me, but only in the fact that it actually came out. Normally, football has a habit of keeping these sorts of things quiet. But he's not the only one. For sure, there are others. Sam is the one who got caught by undercover reporters. I reckon there are untold managers doing a sneaky, getting involved in some action on the side. Am I surprised about what happened with Sam and Mark Curtis? No. We all hear a few stories. Just look at it. Mark Curtis is still, at the time of writing, Sam's agent after all these years. I'm sure I'm not the only one who has been involved in that sort of deal. So it didn't surprise me at all.

I don't think Arsenal did anything wrong. They got a good deal out of it. They got me for a small fee. They were happy to go along with it. If Sky was doing it from the outset, then I would probably have got a better contract for myself. When I first turned pro, the contract wasn't amazing. It was one drawn up after a deal struck by Mark Curtis, who wasn't my agent. But you have to remember that I was getting £45 a week in a brown envelope at Notts

County. I was not old enough to be on the YTS or go through the system, so they had to pay me in cash. I was still supposed to be at school. To me back then, £45 was a lot. Then, suddenly, I was on £750 a week at Arsenal. But if Sky had done the deal, then it would have been a better one for me, for sure. So Arsenal got me cheaply. They were happy with it and *everyone* was happy with it. Everyone got something on the back of my being a youngster and not really being able to have a say or know what was going on.

I never saw Mark Curtis again after that. It was wham, bam and that was it. It was like a one-night stand, which I've had many of!

Sam Allardyce ended up on the front page, just as Mark Curtis did, because it was a sting. There was my dad with a wad of money in a service-station car park and it was all a big setup. I've got to be honest: I was oblivious to it all.

But that's what still happens a lot, yet the difference was that it was a sting. The papers had it all and they could run the story. It's never going to stop in football, either, just because Sam got caught out. Now they might be a bit wiser. Sam got caught out meeting some so-called investors, but, while that put some people off or warned them to be more careful, it won't stop it. And then you wonder why you can't get a move. It's because everyone wants to get paid.

I've never been turned over by people I know. Sky has always been honest and tried to do his best for me. But I have known other agents – and there are foreign agents I don't know – trying to get illegal payments, bungs, call them what you like. One agent trying to set me up with a move to Dubai was demanding 75 per cent of Sky's fee and he wanted 10 per cent of my wages. If I was getting £500,000, then I would have to give him 10 per cent of that. We said no and, next thing, there's no deal on the table.

You start off by talking about the deal and the team, and, if you don't agree, then the deal's off the table. It goes on all over the world. If people aren't getting paid, then the deal is not happening.

I had no idea that my dad had worn a wire and taped the conversation with Mark Curtis, but that was probably the only way you could ever prove something like that had gone on. It's incredible when you think about it.

I remember going to Arsenal and we didn't even negotiate. These were the terms, the contract was put on the table and I just signed it. Liam Brady dealt with it all.

When I was at Arsenal, Liam Brady and Don Howe were a massive part of my younger years growing up and getting into the club. I didn't have too much to do with Arsène Wenger while I was growing up. You sign a contract, turn pro at seventeen, and it was difficult to take it all in. I remember at one point thinking, 'Wow – am I that good?' I was in the local paper, on the fronts of all the national papers. I remember being on the train and trying to catch the guy's eye – the one who was reading the paper opposite me – thinking to myself, 'You see that guy on the front of the paper? That's me!'

It was amazing at first, then it fizzles out. You get used

to it and I didn't let it go to my head. I took it in my stride and didn't think much of it. One of my weaknesses is that I don't think I'm different from the guy who works in McDonald's. I forget I'm in the public eye and I can't always behave like Tom, Dick or Harry and get away with it. You can't do that if you're a footballer. That's when I get into trouble. I think of myself as a normal guy, but you just can't do that. You get paid a lot and you forget that all eyes are on you. Maybe it's a good thing in some ways but it also means you come unstuck and you get into trouble.

I liked the attention at first, as any kid would. As I saw myself on the front page of the paper on the train, I was tapping my dad on the shoulder saying, 'Dad, that's me!' I'd stayed in London for three days, in the hotel, signed and had then come back.

To this day, that is probably one of my biggest regrets. I was naïve. I didn't ask questions, didn't think about it, I just signed. I should never have signed for Arsenal at that stage. I should have stayed at Notts County. I was fifteen years of age, coming up to my sixteenth birthday. I would have been playing in the first team, or been in the first-team squad at least, maybe been on the bench, and I would have been a pro. I would have been comfortable at home with my family, my friends – very comfortable.

I would have been playing first-team football at such a young age. I would still be in the shop window but I would have also been playing regularly, progressing and learning a lot more through first-team football, whatever level I was at.

I went to a big club and got lost. If I'd stayed at Notts County, people would have said, 'He's only sixteen, doing well.' When I went to Arsenal, I played in the League Cup at sixteen and I was the youngest at the time until Cesc Fàbregas broke it.

But after that, I didn't play regularly until I was twenty-one. That's a big chunk of my career lost from sixteen to twenty-one and I was just going through the motions. I was stuck in the youth team, getting frustrated. I was feeling so frustrated.

GARY PENNANT: He was the world's most expensive teenager at the time. At the time I think he would have made it but I think it was Ray Parlour in his position and Ray Parlour was very different. He was very hardworking. Whereas Arsenal had all their flair players, Ray Parlour was a workhorse in comparison.

He was the one who blocked Jermaine. Even when Jermaine scored a hat-trick against Southampton, I thought, 'Right, here's his chance.' But he still didn't get a chance. I can see that must have been disheartening for him.

My upbringing and my disciplinary record made it look as if it was going one way. I didn't get the support, the upbringing of a normal person who could handle a few setbacks and disappointments. I didn't, and I couldn't, handle it. I would fly off the handle, lose my temper and get very frustrated very easily. I'm not patient. That's not me, unfortunately.

I should have stayed at Notts County, stayed there for another couple of seasons until I was eighteen or something, got some experience under my belt, improved and got a structure going for my career. I would've played a lot of first-team football. And yet I just got lost at Arsenal and I went off the rails a bit.

I had all this talk, all this stuff about being a big talent, all the hype – and then, suddenly, nothing.

* * *

Then I got homesick, I started coming home every week and my friends back in Nottingham were saying, 'It's amazing you've signed for Arsenal.' But it didn't feel like that.

I was going back every weekend, living it up in Nottingham, and here I was, the Premier League footballer, hanging out with all my old mates from the Meadows getting into all sorts of bother.

There was one incident that I will never forget, one that I certainly didn't tell Arsenal about. I had the luckiest escape of my life – but one of my friends was not so lucky. We were in a car. I was with a girl in the back. There was a girl in the passenger side with another mate, Christopher Joseph, who had looked out for me when it all kicked off near the KFC a couple of years earlier. We had been to a club and on the way back we saw this car behind us with no lights on. So we thought, 'This is strange.' Then, next thing we know, this car came speeding past, came in front of us and tried to ram us. My mate was driving like Lewis Hamilton, trying to swerve and get out of the way. He was driving his mum's brand-new Peugeot 206. Brand-new car, night out, birds in the car, perfect. Then, next thing you know, we're being practically rammed off the road.

Luckily, we escaped unscathed – the car did not. But, if they had managed to stop us, we'd have been in a lot of trouble.

Another one of my friends, Benjamin Smith, got caught in a different area: St Ann's. He was with three guys but there were about ten from St Ann's who caught Ben, and he got stabbed for being in the wrong area. They stabbed him about twelve to fifteen times. He has to take tablets for the rest of his life. They carved 'ST' into his cheek with a knife. He got caught on enemy territory. It was as simple as that.

It was a really big scar. It was 'ST' for St Ann's. I remember his mum calling me, asking me to go and visit him in hospital, where he was in a coma. She said that he spoke highly of me and if I spoke to him maybe it would help him wake up. It was a sad, sad time.

I was about seventeen and at Arsenal then. I kept that

quiet when I went to visit him! It was very sad at the time and it was tough for his family. His mum was phoning me and it was hard to take it all in.

It was touch and go for him. He's still in good spirits, though. Maybe he knows that he's lucky to be alive and is being grateful to have survived.

I know that if those lads who chased us had caught our car, it wouldn't have been a pretty sight. We have a pretty good idea of what would have happened. So it's thanks to Chris and his lunatic driving. The problem was that we were in a different place because we'd been to a club and were driving home. We had basically gone onto the wrong estate and were in the wrong area. That's what happens when you go onto someone else's turf. Luckily, we escaped and as soon as we turned into Meadows, they had to stop because they wouldn't go in there and they just drove on.

The next day, Chris tried to stop his mum from finding out about the damage to her brand-new car, tried to keep it on the hush-hush, but the car had some big dents in it. Then she went mental! He had to come clean. She said, 'You're not driving it ever again!' We saw the funny side of that, but not at the time.

I still see him and the old crowd when I go back to Nottingham. I was good friends with Wes Morgan, too, who grew up in Nottingham and went on to help Leicester win the Premier League. I went on a stag do with Wes and all that crowd not so long back and Wes paid for them all. He was a year younger, and as we all got older we went our separate ways, but we're still in touch. He didn't really move away from the area because he signed for Nottingham Forest and he's still at Leicester at the time of writing.

That was at the time when I was coming back and forth from Arsenal because I couldn't really settle and I was missing Nottingham. It was a crazy time. When I was in London, it was like a bubble because you live differently as a professional footballer in this different world. But, as soon as I went back to Nottingham, I was in my comfort zone. The further you progress in your career, the more you have to make adjustments. You have to do things differently. You can't put yourself in situations where you get into trouble. You're in the public eye and you want to progress, but, if you're constantly in trouble, it's no good if you want to reach the top level.

I don't think my mates in Nottingham understood at the time and would give me some stick. They used to say stuff like, 'You've forgotten your friends; you go to London; you never come back; you think you've made it, so forget us.' I think they probably understand better now. My mates were pissed off. It was hard, because I do miss them to this day, and people do drift anyway. Everyone grows up, some get married, settle down and have children. You see less of them.

For me, it was different because of being associated with gangs, gang members and certain people. I'm not saying it looks bad, because they're still my friends, but I probably didn't need the headache and the headlines because I was getting into enough trouble anyway just by being on my own. It was a hard choice, but I had to have less to do with my friends back in Nottingham. It was so tough, because in my heart all I wanted was to be with my friends and yet I was also having to think about my career.

* * *

I got to eighteen and started to blend in a bit more. I became close friends with Ashley Cole and Paulo Vernazza, who, to this day, is still one of my best mates.

I made new mates, started seeing the kind of life that I was not used to. I had been at Notts County, been at Nottingham, and suddenly here I was in London, enjoying it, going home less and less. I saw less of mates I'd grown up with. I drifted away from my home, I drifted away from my dad, and I was scared at that point that it would come out and embarrass me.

I gradually cut my ties from Nottingham, moved to London and really got into the way of life.

I was in digs for a while and then I moved in with my auntie Diane. She moved to London, started a life in the city, and when I went down there she invited me to live with her.

But even that went wrong! Arsenal paid the rent for a year, but my family were never good with money. They put the money in my auntie's account and my auntie, her fella, her daughter and I lived in this house that the club rented.

They paid the rent for the year, but my auntie spent half of it! I remember one time how she was upset, embarrassed, and I never knew why. She had to come clean, because the rent wasn't being paid, and the word got back to Arsenal and it ended up with my having to pay the rent and also pay the club some money back as well.

It was good living in that house, because I'd had no privacy growing up, and this was the first time I'd had my own bedroom. When I grew up with my father, I had a bedroom but it wasn't *much* of a bedroom. I had a bed but there were no carpets. It had old floorboards and you could see down the slits. It didn't have wallpaper, had no curtains, and it was all very basic.

It felt great to be in a house. I felt proud because, even when we'd moved to a new location before, when my brother was about eight, I was thirteen, it was *his* room because the wallpaper depicted baby dinosaurs, and he had one of those beds that are shaped like a car. I had two mattresses on the floor. He had a wardrobe; my clothes were scattered. Part of that was down to me because I've never been tidy!

However, being in London, having my own room, earning a good wage, was all new to me. I remember those early days at Arsenal well. Don Howe was a great coach, Liam Brady was head of youth development, and Neil Banfield and Don Givens were the coaching staff.

Howe was such a really great guy. I really respected him. I was very grateful and felt very honoured to work under him.

I think that, when it came to developing my game, my crossing was probably self-taught. When I got better, people tried to copy me and others were asking me, 'How are you doing that?' I was copying and learning from David Beckham, as we saw earlier, because it looked so good. Being a winger, I was getting down the wing, getting to the by-line and floating it in. I'd watched Beckham and suddenly I was whipping the ball in. You didn't need to beat the man: you could put it in from a standing position; you could give it proper whip and really exaggerate it. You obviously have to have the technique, which I definitely had, but it's mastering it, the body shape, how to come around the ball, and that's what I basically learned and mastered.

The art of crossing, I think, has vanished. The game is more intricate. People want to be like Barcelona, passing it and not whipping in balls. It's more intricate, tapping it around the box, one-twos and through balls. The crossing has come out of the game. There are still players out there who can do it, but in the modern game it's not really used as much. You don't see as many big centre forwards, such as a Ruud van Nistelrooy or a Peter Crouch, not many tall players in the box.

I felt I was making great progress, but the frustration I felt inside was massive. I went from being £2 million *wunderkind*, the next big thing. I understood that I was only sixteen, couldn't go straight in, and I was going to play some youth team first team. But it just dragged on and on. If they'd put me in a bit earlier, even if they'd put me in training with the first team instead of keeping me in the academy until I was eighteen or nineteen, it would have been a different story. I'd have got that professionalism and respect. But being stuck in the youth team was bad for me. Youth team football in those days was still doing chores and training, but it was all about fun.

Because of all the hype when I moved and signed for Arsenal, I was thinking, 'When am I going to get my chance?' I just got so frustrated. I'm sure if I saw Arsène now then he might admit a little mistake. He could have put me in the first-team changing rooms, not to be playing, but for the experience of being *with* the first team. If such a situation happened now, you wouldn't get a sixteen-year-old signing for a record fee. They would go into the first-team setup rather than change in the academy.

The frustration took a while to kick in. The first year I got there, I was still adapting to life. I was settling in at Arsenal, going home to Nottingham every weekend and that kind of took up all of my energy.

* * *

It was when I started not going back home as much that I began my life in London, making friends there, starting to go out with Paolo Vernazza and Ashley Cole, starting to think about things and get fed up. That was when the frustration really crept in. Ashley was playing first team. I can remember Arsène saying to me that he always put me against Ashley Cole in training on purpose. Ashley and I would never be on the same team. He said I was the only player who could give him problems and it was good for me. But putting me against Ashley was a kick in the teeth in a way, because I was thinking, 'If that's the case, then why am I not in the first-team squad?' There were no better left-backs out there at the time.

SKY ANDREW: It was definitely the right place at the wrong time. Arsenal is a great club but no one knew Jermaine's situation, his upbringing, and he'd had a difficult childhood. His reading and writing were very basic. He had grown up in such a tough part of town, was very rough and ready. There were certain basic things that he didn't know how to do. There are basic things, which everyone takes for granted, silly stuff like taking a shower, communicating with people and so on. You've got to understand that he was left to his own devices. He would wander around, he could leave the house for two days and no one would notice. He was left on his own. He had no one. But people didn't really care about him, they just wanted to get a deal done. I'm not talking about Arsenal. It was people trying to earn out of a transfer. It was wrong.

Jermaine carries that monkey on his back, for sure. If he'd stayed until the end of the season, he'd have been a different character and even staying for that short space of time would have helped mould his character differently.

I think the move too soon affected him and made him far more reckless as an individual.

It was something that he just wasn't prepared for. He wasn't prepared for the whole spotlight. He had been an unknown kid in Nottingham and then suddenly he's in the limelight as a record transfer for a fifteen-year-old. All of that gave him attention.

Some people would think, 'That's cool.' But it affected him in a really negative way. He was still a kid moving from one club to another. He was no super-duper kid. He was a good player, a good talent, but the pressure of his moving – £2 million – to a club like Arsenal got to him, and, if things had been done in a different way and there had been a natural transition, it wouldn't have been so bad. But as soon as he got there, people were expecting big things, for him to play straightaway, and Arsenal were getting questions at every press conference about how they were going to deal with him.

Liam Brady loved him, Arsène Wenger loved him, David Dein, who was the vice-chair, loved him. I remember David Dein saying such great things about him – but his upbringing, the way he grew up, he really struggled with his new life. He just wasn't ready. All the mistakes he made were down to his recklessness.

He was taken out of his home surroundings, put into the spotlight and maybe that has contributed to this piece of his personality that makes him so reckless.

I was still young, I found it hard to talk to Arsène Wenger about my frustrations because of his stature in the game. He was physically a big guy, and his accent, the way he talks to you, was daunting at times. When he had players such as Patrick Vieira, Emmanuel Petit, Freddie Ljungberg and Ray Parlour, how could I knock on the door and say, 'Why aren't I in the team, boss?'

They were great, those guys, to me, especially Patrick. He was hard on me, but he was good. I could tell that he liked me generally as a person and as a player. He was hard on me because I think he wanted me to do well. I think Patrick will be a really good coach, definitely. He's got that character, that personality, and that's why he was such a great captain at Arsenal. He can lead and, when he leads, other people will follow.

* * *

I was getting nibbles of the first team – in the cups, being on the bench for the Champions League – and so it was getting closer. I remember one game at Highbury. We were winning 2–0 and I could see that the manager was bringing on a sub, Lee Dixon, at right midfield, and I just lost my head and was thinking, 'Is he winding me up?'

After the game, you are getting changed, are still fuming. You want to swear. You are really upset, huffing and puffing. And that's not good for the team. People can see that you're upset, that you're pissed off. Then next day in training, you are thinking, 'Why am I training? Why am I bothering? What's the point of trying and working like a madman?' I felt as if I'd lost my way around then. I was getting really downhearted.

I know that I won't get much sympathy, because I'd signed for a big club, one of the biggest clubs in the world, for big money. But all I wanted to do was play football and I felt as if I didn't ever get a chance to do what I most loved in all the world.

And that frustration, given time, completely overwhelmed me and shaped everything that went wrong for me at Arsenal from that point on.

CHAPTER 4

A NIGHT TO REMEMBER

My first start for Arsenal in the Premier League was on 7 May 2003. It was against Southampton and it was a night I will never forget – but not just because I scored a hat-trick.

The previous night I went to a party organised by the lifestyle mag *FHM*, got wasted, incredibly drunk, stayed out all night and woke up with a McDonald's breakfast! It was the worst possible preparation. I felt like being sick through the game and yet it was the best game of my entire Arsenal career. Typical, really!

Basically, the day before a game, we had a training session that we were all in for. The manager named the squad as usual on that day. On this occasion, I was in the squad. I knew Ashley Cole and all the other boys were being rested and had a day off. They only had to report for the game, show their faces, but they had a day off.

MENTAL

I was close mates with Ashley, Jermaine Wynter and Paolo Vernazza and we all lived nearby in a nice estate called Princess Park Manor. There were lots of players there, some pop stars, and it was a great place to be. After training one day, we all went round to someone's house. All the other lads were up for going out and I just said, 'I'm coming.'

They all said I couldn't, I was playing, don't be stupid. But I just thought I'd be on the bench as usual because Ray Parlour, Robert Pirès and Freddie Ljungberg were in the squad. They were all going to the *FHM* party and I was going crazy. 'I *am* coming to this!' They were getting angry with me, threatening to lock me in. I said I'd just climb out of the window, get a taxi and go to the party. They were getting really angry with me by now, particularly Ashley, calling me a dickhead, stupid, and telling me there would be other parties.

But I wouldn't be told. I knew there were going to be so many girls there. I was determined to go. There was no way that I *wasn't* going.

I promised not to drink, not to have a drop. So I went there, it was a good night – and I ended up getting completely wasted! We got so wasted they forgot about my having a game the next day.

JON FORTUNE: We all lived in Princess Park Manor, a complex of flats in north London. I had a flat there, Jermaine was there, everyone was young, free and single. It was a plush place to live. Ashley Cole had a flat in the Docklands area. He wasn't involved in the game, so was given a night off and was up for a big night. He was getting changed for a big night out at this *FHM* party. Jermaine just couldn't say no. He was begging to come out. Ashley kept saying, 'Trust me, don't do it, you might be playing.' Jermaine was thinking he wouldn't and was desperate to come.

We made this plan to lock him in. We tried everything to lock him in the flat! We locked him in rooms, locked the front door, and yet somehow he kept escaping. He was like a dog waiting by the front door to be let out! First he got out and was waiting by the front door, then was waiting for us by the taxi. He just wouldn't give up.

Eventually, he just ignored us and came along. It was the old Emporium, a decent party; we were young, enjoying ourselves. We left late and he was still there at 4 a.m. Then we went back to the flats and he was still up with a girl until 5 a.m. I remember waking up and there he was having a McDonald's breakfast – a double-sausage-and-egg muffin or whatever.

SKY ANDREW: I didn't know until years later. I became the father figure to this lad. If I walked into a room, he would stop talking. He was a bit scared of me. People would tell me stories and I wouldn't believe it in the beginning. When he scored the hat-trick against Southampton – bam, bam, bam – it was amazing. Then people told me he'd gone out, he'd been drunk. And Jermaine only told me a long time afterwards.

They tried to lock him in, Ashley, Jon Fortune and Paolo Vernazza, but he got out and scored the hat-trick drunk. He set records with that hat-trick – but he was also drunk. It was incredible.

We had to meet at the Four Seasons hotel at Canary Wharf. We had to report at 11 a.m. I reported for the game, went to the hotel, had a pre-match meal and, after the meeting, the manager was giving out the team. I was drinking a bottle of water, trying to rehydrate because I was so hungover. I was sitting at the back. The manager had his whiteboard and there was a piece of paper over it. He lifts the paper, folds it over the back and it shows the team.

I looked to who was on the bench. I was so used to looking and finding myself on the substitutes' bench. My name wasn't there – and my heart started beating. I looked at the squad, I saw my name on the right, and my heart dropped into my stomach. I was thinking 'Why now? Why are you starting me now!'

As soon as I saw my name, I glugged the litre of water all down. Through the day, I must have drunk four litres of water. I was now shitting myself. It was my big chance and if I performed really badly they'd rumble me. I was thinking, 'Oh, shit! I've blown it.'

I was so nervous, I got on the pitch and still felt awful, still felt so hung over. But there was something in me. I felt as if I was going to die, but I put everything into it, every bit of power I had, every bit of concentration and energy, I put into that, no matter how much I was hurting.

No one suspected. No one knew. No one knew anything, no one even said I smelled of alcohol. I wasn't breathing near anyone. I was avoiding everyone, standing on the other side of the room, opposite everyone.

The game kicked off. I was running around and I was just hoping for it to be half-time! Then I score. Thierry Henry played me in, I hit it in the bottom corner and I was just thinking, 'Thank you, God!' Then I was celebrating. I looked over to the bench and I was just willing someone to substitute for me. I was so happy and I was thinking, 'Bring me off!' Then another went in. When the second one went in, I was thinking, 'I wonder what the other boys are thinking!' I wonder if they know I've scored two goals.

Then I completed a hat-trick and I was thinking, 'This is not real.' I couldn't believe it. I didn't tell a soul. The only two who knew were Ashley and Paolo, whom I was out with. I didn't even tell Sky. In fact, I didn't tell Sky for years afterwards. I got the match ball after that. But, during the last twenty minutes, I was feeling as if I was going to puke because the alcohol was still in my body. I felt awful! I was like, 'Get me off – please!'

JON FORTUNE: I had an awards night that evening, rang Coley on the way there. We arranged to speak later on and have another night out. I rang him after the awards and Ashley just said, 'Jon, you won't believe what I've just seen: Pennant has just scored a hat-trick!' I couldn't believe he even started the game, let alone score a hat-trick.

I actually think it had big implications for his career. He has the big night out, gets up, eats a McDonald's breakfast and still scores a hat-trick. He's a teenager, plays in the Premier League and thinks, 'This is easy.' It's a fun story, but it had bigger consequences. If he'd been sick at half-time, unable to carry on, he would have learned his lesson. But if he does that, scores a hat-trick, then he will do it again.

He never shows what he has been through; he never lets slip what's happened to him.

He had a big entourage around him and that's not always a good thing. You need friends, not hangers-on. You need honest people who wouldn't be afraid to say no to him, to keep him out of trouble or to stop him going out.

There was another funny story from when I got caught after another night out. We went to a boat party. Katie Price was there, all over Ashley. Linsey Dawn McKenzie was there.

I pulled two birds. I went home. It was fairly local. I remember saying, 'I've got to be in training for 9 a.m.'

I woke up in the morning and still had my clothes on from the night out. These two girls got in the car, drove me to training, and I tried to sneak in. The girls were in the front of the car, I was in the back. They stopped nearby and got out, miniskirts, high heels, half-nine in the morning, and I think Arsène Wenger saw it because he didn't say anything to me, but he called my agent and was upset. He said, 'Jermaine is not living right, I saw him with two girls straight from a nightclub.' I thought I'd been sneaky enough to get away with it, but nothing gets past Arsène!

He wasn't always a great communicator. He doesn't like confrontation, not at all. He rarely gets angry. If he gets angry in the changing room, it's for a big reason. He will say a few words and that's it. He will shout, 'This is not right – stop it!' There's no effing and blinding, just a few words, a little explosion, and that's it.

Mind you, I didn't half give him cause for concern sometimes. We were at training one day. I was nineteen and there was one hell of a squad, Thierry, Patrick and the rest. Then, one day, as we're finishing up training, Arsène Wenger sends some of the staff to come and get me, saying that the police were there to see me, that they'd come from Nottingham.

I'm thinking: 'What have I done now?' I've been a good boy for six months! They looked worried, and I was thinking:

MENTAL

'What it is?' Someone told me to go into Arsène's office. I sat down and they spoke to me and told me 'Don't be alarmed, but you could possibly be in danger…'

I was thinking 'Er, OK…' They told me 'We've found a satchel, a bag, and your picture was in it, along with a gun. So we're trying to determine of it's a hit on yourself or whatever.' I'm thinking 'Jesus – someone is going to whack me!'

I got scared, seriously scared. I was genuinely shitting myself. Then I began to think 'What must Arsenal be thinking?' They must be thinking they've signed a lunatic.

I was in my full training kit, the full lot. I'd been having a runaround with Patrick Vieira, Thierry Henry and the next minute I'm being interviewed by the police about being a victim of a gangland hit! Excuse me, Thierry, I'm just about to talk to the police about some guns!

I phoned a mate, my nephew, from home – I better not say who! – and said 'Mate, I think I'm in trouble. Someone is looking to put a hit on me, they've found a bag with a picture of me and a gun in it.'

He's gone 'What sort of bag is it?' I told him it was a Nike bag and suddenly he's going 'Oh, shit! Yeah, yeah, sorry about that bro' – the house got raided and they found the bag that you gave me.' I was sponsored by Nike, and they gave me a big Nike bag full of tracksuits, trainers and kit and I gave it to my mates back home. They took all the stuff, then used the bag to store a gun, but forgot to take out the picture. So the house has been raided and the police found a picture of me and the gun and they're thinking: 'These are gangsters and they've ordered a hit on a footballor.'

My friends were laughing and saying sorry, but the police turned up at the training ground and I couldn't tell Arsenal. 'Sorry – it was just my mates messing about with guns!' So, to this day, I've never told anyone there. Arsène was worried at the time and wondered what they'd let themselves in for! I was training with the first team, it was about 2002, and suddenly he had a player mixed up with guns and gangs...

The police said that they would notify the London section and make sure that I was safe because they were worried that people could follow me to and from training. They told me to keep my eye out when I was going back and forth to the training ground.

The story of my life – sometimes the truth is stranger than fiction. It was a weird feeling with the police coming to the training ground, and I'm wondering what's going through their heads. They obviously never found out the actual truth, so I had to play along with it.

* * *

During the Arsenal days, we had some fantastic times – great nights out, parties, showbiz. It was a proper little soap opera we had going, particularly because we were all living in Princess Park Manor in north London. All the boys lived in there, Girls Aloud lived there as well and it was how Ashley Cole first met Cheryl Cole, whom he later married – but not before some drama.

I remember in 2004, Ashley had just had a brilliant Euros that summer, having played amazingly against Portugal and Cristiano Ronaldo, despite having lost on penalties. But Ashley took a penalty and scored – he did his bit. He had a great tournament.

I was on holiday, watching the game, cheering him on, and when he got back we were all having a game of tennis on the courts in the complex. Ashley, Jon Fortune, Jermaine Wynter and I were having a little knock-around. We would always see the Girls Aloud lot drive in and out; we'd always have a bit of a laugh, shout and say, 'They're looking all right!'

Then, one day, they pulled up while we were playing tennis. We stopped, had a look and thought, 'What's going on here?'

They got out and came across, and it was the ginger nut, Kimberley Walsh, and Cheryl. Cheryl was the loud one. She came across and started saying, 'Well done, Ashley, brilliant Euros, unlucky . . .' And so on. Ashley was loving it. That was how they first started talking.

Further on down the line, they'd swapped numbers, been texting, met up a couple of times. They'd told us all to keep it quiet. Then, one day, Cheryl was round his place, in his apartment with him. The door was locked from the inside. He'd also kept the key in the lock so no one could get in. His girlfriend at the time, Emily, had a key. She came round and she was trying to get in but couldn't. She was calling him, going mad because she knew someone was in there. She had a suspicion that he was in there, up to no good, and she was calling all the lads, going mad, and we were ignoring all her calls because we knew what was going down.

Cheryl and Ashley inside were probably looking at each other thinking, 'What's going on?'

Then, the next day, I was talking to Ashley, who said there'd been no chance he was going to answer the door. No chance whatsoever. Then, a couple of days later, stories came out about it. Ashley couldn't believe it because the only people who knew were Cheryl in the house and Ashley himself, and he'd told Jermaine Wynter and had told me.

I was like, 'It's not going to be Wynts. It definitely wasn't me – what would I gain from that?' Then I just thought it must be Cheryl. Their band were just getting going, they wanted publicity. I said to Ash, 'It must have been her.' He was convinced that it wasn't.

Then I rang Wynts the next day. He was close to Cheryl. He would hang out with her. He was round Cheryl's apartment. He put me on loudspeaker, but I didn't know. So I was just talking to him as a mate and I was going, 'It's definitely not me or you. It's definitely Cheryl!' He's round her apartment, he's got me on loudspeaker and I'm going, 'It's her, it's her. Who the fuck are Girls Aloud? They're shit. They need all the publicity they can get. It's definitely her. It's one hundred per cent her to get their names in the paper. It's definitely her. It definitely wasn't me, so it must be Cheryl, then.' He's saying he wasn't sure it was her and I was still piling in and saying, 'They're shit. She's done it to get publicity, get herself famous and get in the charts. Make a name for themselves, they're brand new, it's definitely her.' I still didn't know I was on loudspeaker.

She was obviously hacked off, had gone back to Ash and kicked off over what I'd said. Ash was then a bit funny with me and I couldn't understand why, because at that stage I still didn't know I'd be on loudspeaker.

Then they all went out. The boys went out separately and we all met up later. I kicked off at Jermaine. 'What's going on? Why haven't you got my back?'

Then Ash was having a go and Cheryl piled in before Jermaine said, 'Mate – you were on loudspeaker!' I looked at Jermaine and I was saying to my mate, 'You prick! Why didn't you take me *off* loudspeaker?'

We didn't speak for about two weeks. It was very off, and everyone fell out for a bit. We didn't ever find out who it was but I think we all assumed. Things moved on and then Ash and Cheryl became official. The rest is history.

* * *

Around that time, I was messaging Kimberley Walsh. She'd always had a boyfriend and is now married to him, but at the time I got her number from Jermaine because he was friends with them all. We would see them whilst we were out, I would flirt, have a little dance, and I said to Jermaine, 'Mate – get me her number – I'm going to graft my nuts off on this one!' I got her number, I was sending her texts, telling her she was amazing, beautiful. She would always say, 'I've got a boyfriend.' But I never gave up, kept trying, but nothing ever came of it. I tried all sorts! I thought she was the one.

It was soon after that I went up North, played for different clubs and I was never around when Cheryl was on the scene. So I don't know whether she's forgiven me or not. I didn't go to the wedding. I think I was in Spain when they got married but we moved on.

JON FORTUNE: I remember when he was at Arsenal, he was such a good player and yet he had Freddie Ljungberg in front of him. When you're talented, you're working hard and trying and still not getting in, then you lose faith, give up, and that's when you go off the rails. Start going out, eating the wrong things, drinking, and if your mindset is wrong then you lose your way.

There was a game at Everton. I wasn't in the squad. I lost a bit of heart, went to the bar, ordered a Coke, was about to order a Jack Daniel's to put in it and then I got a tap on the shoulder and it was the first-team coach, Mervyn Day, telling me I was needed in the dressing room. Not only that, I was starting the game. I'd gone from not being involved to starting and I was a whisker away from having a drink. If that gets smelled on you, you get into trouble and it all goes wrong. I got away with it and Pennant would always get caught out. That's how his luck is and how it worked out for him.

But he wouldn't live his life right, to be honest. I remember a former teammate of his, Jerome Thomas, telling me a story about how they'd blown all their money on a flash car, an Audi TT or something. They didn't have enough money for food and ended up taking the car seats out of the car to scramble around on the floor to look for some change so they could go to McDonald's. It was the day before pay day and they'd spent every last penny.

I know I could have done better at Arsenal, but I did like Arsène, still do. But I still feel I could have been treated better, been given a better shot at succeeding. I think he could have put me in a bit earlier and I am sure that, if I sat down with him, he'd say the same thing.

But I don't have a single bad word to say about Arsène, unlike other managers we'll mention. I do still like him. He's incredibly friendly, polite and a nice guy. Even now when I see him he will still say hello and say, 'Jermaine, how are you?' I know that when other managers have enquired, talked about signing me, then he's had only good things to say about me as a person and as a player.

Most people who come across me do warm to me, because I'm a nice person at heart. Listen, if I read about myself, believed everything, then I probably wouldn't like the way I sounded! I would probably think, 'What an absolute lunatic!' But once you get to sit down with me, get to know me on a better level than that of the crimes and misdemeanours, you see me as a different person.

KEVIN JAMES, FORMER CHARLTON MIDFIELDER AND FRIEND: Jermaine won the FA Youth Cup twice, was part of one of the best youth teams of all time, and it was full of characters.

He's a real talent, but he's also got a great heart. I was doing some work as an academy coach, coaching the kids, and then I got him on the phone, put it on the loudspeaker and played it to all the kids. He was great, told them to enjoy it, gave them some advice, and I think it did have an effect.

My biggest memory of Arsène was when he moved me into the first team's dressing room. He told me that I'd earned it. He sat me down, told me I was a great talent and then challenged me to show how good I was in the first team. He was a good coach, too, took all the training sessions.

MENTAL

But there's one thing for sure: Wenger doesn't like confrontation. I remember in training once that Thierry Henry was playing in a small-sided game. It happens a lot when the ref or the coach calls it out. Someone keeps missing, someone has three touches in a two-touch game. With Thierry, he was having one of those days. Someone had annoyed him or the training kept breaking down. Thierry then got so annoyed that, when the ball came to him, he just booted it into another field. Thierry could sulk if things weren't going his way. But what could you say to him? After all, it's Thierry Henry.

I remember Arsène turning to him after he'd booted the ball into another field and shouting, 'Thierry, stop being a baby!' Thierry just shouted straight back, in French, 'Fuck off!' Then he just marched straight in.

I was thinking, 'Fucking hell!' Jesus! He's just told Arsène Wenger to fuck off – and then walked in! I felt scared around Thierry sometimes. If you didn't give him the ball then he would moan at you, shout at you, and, if you went long, he would go absolutely mental. He could also sulk. My God, could he sulk!

Wenger didn't pull him up on it. He just got on with the job. No way did he do anything about being told to fuck off. Next day, training as usual. Saturday, Thierry scored two goals.

Seeing what he did day to day, I've got to say Thierry Henry is the best player I've ever played with. It was close, though, because Dennis Bergkamp was incredible as well.

And Steven Gerrard. The thing that takes Thierry away from Bergkamp is that Thierry had pace and that pace was frightening. But, ability-wise, Bergkamp was outrageous, while, in training, Henry was incredible. He was so strong. Very few have got that sort of physical strength and power. But only the greats have skill as well, and that's why Thierry is up there with the very, very best. He had everything. Steven Gerrard was captain of Liverpool. But watching Thierry every day, it had to be him. There was a lot of good contenders, because I've played with some great, great players. For me to put Thierry above everyone else says so much about him.

Thierry was also a friend to me at Arsenal. We got on really well. He, Ashley Cole and I would always sit in the same little corner in the changing rooms at training. We would have the same banter, enjoy the same stuff. And Henry was always on a level with me.

I think he will make a good manager. He will definitely be passionate. I can see that playing under him would be a nightmare! He will never be one of those cool, calm, collected managers. That's for sure. But top footballers do make good managers, because they've played the game, so they know what it's like. If he gets a manager's job, then I'll have to see if he wants to sign me up!

Management is a tough game, but the key is being a good man manager. These days, if you're not a yes-man, not a yes-boy, then you get dropped – and it's sad. Other people misbehave and they seem to get away with it.

MENTAL

Funnily enough, the worst player I've ever played with, Igors Stepanovs, was also at Arsenal. He was far and away the worst. Stepanovs came on trial and in training he was good on the ball, bringing it out, confident, and we thought he would continue be good. Then, when we signed him, he just went to pot!

All the pace had gone, his confidence went, he kept making mistakes, falling over the ball; and, when you were playing a small-sided game, you wanted to play against him! You were hoping he was on the opposition.

He won a league title medal. But, believe me, he *stole* the medal! He didn't win it – he must have paid the gaffer for that! He was talking really slowly, and that, along with the way he played, was so funny. He was atrocious.

Pat Rice and Boro Primorac were there on the coaching staff at Arsenal as well. But Arsène would take the sessions; they would join in, give directions as to what the boss wanted.

Boro was a great character. We would take the mickey out of him all the time. He was a genuinely funny guy. And he never spoke English! He was brilliant. He would come out with one-liners. He would have a tooth pick in all the time, as if he were Pablo Escobar! Absolutely fantastic character.

He read the game for Arsène, sat in the stands and went over the game and tactics and details with a fine-tooth comb. If he felt you were a good player, he would look for strengths and weaknesses; he was really good to me. I really liked him.

But I couldn't really see eye to eye with Pat Rice. I think he had something against me. It felt as though he didn't want me to succeed. He said early on to my agent Sky that I wouldn't make it and then, funnily enough, I was Man of the Match in a Champions League final.

I remember hearing him say I'd never make it, and those sorts of things can really inspire you! I remember talking to Sky after the Champions League final and saying, 'I wonder what Pat Rice is thinking now after watching this.' That was honestly one of my first reactions after the final.

When I left Arsenal for Birmingham, Pat Rice said to Sky, 'Told you he'd never make it.' He didn't say it to my face, just to Sky. He said I didn't have the right attitude. I don't know whether it was jealousy, whether he didn't like me, whatever. But it hurt me – and inspired me as well.

I think Rice was the person I most enjoyed proving wrong. That conversation with Sky, when I left Arsenal after a drink-driving incident, really stuck with me, when he said to Sky that I would never make it, would never make anything of myself. Then, two years later, I was playing in the Champions League final and was thinking inside, 'Yeah, have that.'

I've hardly seen him since. I've seen him when I've played Arsenal but never had the chance to really say something. But I've done that already by proving him wrong.

* * *

I had some really good times out on loan early in my career when I was still at Arsenal. The best time was at Leeds, but before I went there I was at Watford with Paolo Vernazza. He's my best friend. He sorted it out, basically, for me to go to Watford when Gianluca Vialli was the manager.

It was like training with your mates, and playing first-team football. It was a good experience.

I remember going on a pre-season break, a training camp in Spain near La Coruña, with Micah Hyde, Gifton Noel-Williams, Tommy Smith and Heiðar Helguson, and it was a funny trip.

I don't know if we were supposed to go out but, the manager had said we could have a couple of drinks – see you at 11 a.m. for training the next day. We ended up in the middle of nowhere. Then we walked into what we thought was a nightclub – and it was a brothel!

Everyone was in a thong or a see-through dress and we were thinking it was amazing. But then it quickly dawned on us that it was a top-class brothel – as we soon realised when other people kept disappearing!

I had a better time on the pitch at Leeds. Whenever I see fans now they all say, 'Come back to Leeds.' When I was playing in England, I would have loved to have signed for Leeds again, permanently, because it's a massive club in the Championship and the fans are great. It's a great club to play for.

That was a very strange time. Not just playing for the club, but also the experience of going out into the city centre. It was wild. These nights out were huge. I met a girlfriend there. She was at uni. Leeds is full of students. Everyone was just wild and the people there were a good crowd: Gary Kelly, Alan Smith, Mark Viduka, Harry Kewell. . . Harry was a funny guy.

I remember in training once, when Peter Reid was manager, that Mark Viduka was strutting his stuff on the pitch. If he wasn't bothered, he *really* wasn't bothered, and I think Reid wasn't taking any shit. Reid had a go at Viduka in his Australian accent: 'I'm fucking off, I'm fucking off, you lot. If you lot want to get relegated, you stay here with him. But I'm fucking off!' We were all looking at each other, thinking, 'Did that really just happen?'

* * *

It was never dull, but all the time I was at Arsenal, though, I just wanted to make it work, and yet I was getting more and more frustrated.

I regretted going to Arsenal too early in my career. It wasn't the right move for me. It came at the wrong time, and it didn't work. But, once I was there, I was desperate to succeed, and to end up failing like I did was a huge disappointment.

I had six or seven years at Arsenal. The best period was the hat-trick and winning the FA Youth Cup. Those two years were a great development in my career. Every player in the academy looked capable of progressing into the first team. There was so much competition and there were some good memories in there. But some massive regrets, too. And more were to follow.

just before it happened and he could tell that I was in danger of losing my way. He told me that he was happy with my training. I was training well and there were no incidents in six months; he just told me to keep going. I had been frustrated at not playing more, but I trained really hard, kept my head down, and I was working towards getting a new contract.

My agent, Sky Andrew, didn't tell me but he had a meeting and spoke to Arsène, who'd said, 'He's been here for three years, he's done everything he can. We've agreed to give him a new contract.'

I was on about £20,000 a week and then, a week later came my arrest for drink-driving, and that was how I got to go to Birmingham City – and ended up in prison.

I actually didn't find out about the new contract until years later, when Sky told me. I said to him, 'Cheers, Sky. Thanks for that. You could have told me you'd had the conversation so I could be on best behaviour!'

SKY ANDREW: The worst thing, the worst moment, was that we had a contract lined up. If you spoke to David Dein or Arsène Wenger, it was in the top three toughest conversations that I've ever had. Basically, he got into trouble, then I sat him down and said to him, 'You've got to turn your life around.' He had been stopped for drink-driving, then began to behave himself and Wenger and Dein were so impressed with the way that he knuckled down, how hard he worked. We sat down around David Dein's house – David, Arsène and I – and I just went for the both of them. I told them they'd underestimated him. I told them basically that they didn't expect him to respond.

Afterwards, David Dein sent me a message saying they'd never had anyone speak to them like that. They agreed to give him a new contract. I thought, 'Wow – what a turning point!' I phoned him up and said, 'They'll give you a contract. Well done for turning it round.' I was so honest with them because I respected them so much, especially David Dein. The great man wanted the best for his players and, even if they messed up, he would give them a chance. He had the contract there and ready. They were talking about what kind of offer they would make.

I had a year left on my contract at that stage, my head was going – and then it happened. I first got arrested for drink-driving while I was on loan at Leeds in 2004 and I was still banned from driving when I got caught in 2005. To get done again in 2012 is something I'm deeply ashamed of.

In 2004, I got caught doing an illegal U-turn. The police breathalysed me and I was just over the limit, so I got banned for twelve months. Then, a week before that first ban was due to be lifted, I crashed, got caught again and it all went wrong. Horribly wrong.

I'd had a night out with friends. The stupid part of it was that I got a cab home, got in and I was texting a girl, and she wrote, 'I'm staying in this hotel – come over.'

I jumped in a car I'd borrowed – as I remembered it – from Ashley Cole, I didn't even think about it. Again, it was all to do with a woman – the story of my life. On the way, I crashed into a lamppost in Aylesbury. The car was in a bad way: the passenger side was mangled but, luckily, no one was hurt. I tried to drive off, pulling the lamppost with me, before I got pulled over and arrested.

It came out in the press that, because of whose car it was, I'd said I was Ashley Cole! They jumped on that. I didn't say that I was Ashley – I probably didn't because Ashley had a game the next day and it would have got him into trouble! Ashley's car was a Mercedes SL63 AMG, worth a lot of money, and it cost £30,000 to repair. I had to pay and it turned out to be one very expensive night out! He was OK about it. He was obviously pissed off, annoyed, but it didn't break our friendship. He wasn't short of cars at the time.

SKY ANDREW: The thing is, it wasn't even Ashley Cole's car. It was Anthony Gardner's brand-new SL63, worth £110,000. He smashed it up and then told the police he was Ashley Cole. That's really not very clever. He had to pay Anthony Gardner back the full £110,000 in a £10,000 instalment each month. I think he had a problem with depression. The only thing that could get him up was drink. Whenever he had a drink, he would become this fun person who would do anything.

It's an awful experience being arrested. They take you in; they know who you are; straightaway they tell someone, message a friend, and it all goes round. I got to the station; they breathalysed me; I was over the limit. They arrest you, take your laces out, fingerprint you and then throw you in a little cell. Then they basically just leave you to rot.

I was allowed a phone call. I rang my agent, Sky. They wouldn't let me leave until I was under the limit. They said they'd come back in six hours and said they'd test me again. When, finally, you are under the limit they call someone to pick you up.

As we've seen, I've been caught drink-driving three times and on my last one I had to wait sixteen hours before they let me go; it was a very big night!

I've got to admit that I was driving throughout that first drink-drive ban. I used to drive to training at Arsenal. I would leave the car in the car park next door and then walk to the changing rooms as if I'd got a taxi, no one ever knew about it. Everyone assumed I wouldn't be stupid enough. There were never any questions.

But the worst thing was facing up to the shame and the devastation that the ban caused to my life and my career. David Dein, who was Arsenal vice-chair at the time, came round to my place with Sky, telling me that I needed to tell him the whole truth and to try to save my career at the club.

That was a really bad time. I thought I was going to get sacked. I think if I'd been sent down, been sent to prison, I *would* have been sacked. But I think they did a deal with Birmingham to send me there permanently, because that's where I went after the last of the loans – *from* Birmingham *to* Birmingham, so to speak.

It was crazy, but I was about to go to prison, and Arsenal still wanted £3 million: £1 million straight up, £1 million if Birmingham stayed in the Premier League and another £1 million on appearances.

Arsenal, and not making it work, is my biggest regret. That new contract that I found about only afterwards would have put me in among the first-team players. My first contract wasn't massive. When I first signed, it was £1,700 a week, then went up a grand a year. By the time I was nineteen, it was about £3,700. That new contract would have put me in the first-team bracket. I might have been used a bit more, as well.

It was devastating. Maybe if Sky had told me as soon as it'd been talked about, then who knows? But Sky says it was just talks. He'd been begging them for a new contract. And, knowing me, it wouldn't have made a difference.

It's a fantastic club and it's my biggest regret. You never know what might have happened. I could see what had happened to Ashley Cole, and I was hoping to follow in his footsteps. He had a great career, won so much, and yet I do think Arsenal improved me as a player. When I went to Birmingham, when the deal became permanent, it was like a new lifeline and, performance-wise, that's definitely up there with my first season at Liverpool. The permanent basis at Birmingham – not the loan – represented some of the best times. Steve Bruce, the Birmingham manager, was fantastic for me – amazing. No matter what I did, no matter what trouble I got in, he played me and always gave me a chance. He'd just call me his 'bad boy'.

Birmingham was great for me, because I was playing week in, week out. It took my mind off things and I was really enjoying my football, doing well for Steve Bruce, doing well for Birmingham. The fans took to me. It was beginning to click for me. I was scoring goals, doing well, getting Man of the Match.

But, obviously, it's typical of me to nearly blow it all by getting arrested.

I'd gone from being nearly sacked by Arsenal to going to prison, and then the loan move was made permanent. It took my mind off everything and I was really enjoying my football. It really clicked.

There was no backlash at Birmingham when they signed me, even though they were signing someone who had just been convicted and sent to prison for drink-driving. I had played so well at Birmingham while I was there on loan that it was almost seen as a given that they would sign me, no matter the circumstances.

But my bargaining position was weakened. They had me by the balls as well. They made a really low offer because they knew I had no option but to sign. Sky said it was not enough, but there was a bit of toing and froing. They offered peanuts in the beginning. They were saying I'd been to prison, that no other club would touch me, but in the end they made an effort to keep me.

Steve Bruce came to see me in prison and for him to take time out to do that was incredible. He's a big-name manager. I can still see his face as he walked through the prison, and all the attention. 'Look, there's Steve Bruce!' It was incredible and I was so embarrassed. 'Sorry, Gaffer!' But it was a great thing for him to do. He was pictured outside the prison with Sky. It was such a big story at the time.

I remember my trial so clearly. My solicitor told me the woman who'd gone before me had a baby in the back of the car she crashed into another, and they gave her a suspended sentence and ordered her to do community service. I was thinking I would be happy with that. I was thinking she'd get worse because of the baby and the fact that I'd hit a lamppost rather than another car.

I didn't think I was going to go to prison or be sent down. I just didn't think it was possible, especially after that woman before me had done something very similar, but had a baby in the back and got community service. I thought, 'Thank God for that! I'm not going to prison.' I didn't think a custodial sentence was on the cards. I was confident; everyone was confident.

So I was hoping the outcome, after what had been said, would not be too bad. But, when it was time for the verdict, I looked at Sky and they read it out. They said it was going to be a custodial sentence and I was waiting for the 'but' or the punchline with the suspended sentence. But it never came. There I was in the dock and I was being sent to prison for three months!

SKY ANDREW: When he got done for drink driving- again, I just couldn't believe it when I heard. That was a real kick in the teeth for everyone, especially for Arsène and David Dein, because they put their faith in him. I think it was that moment that they decided he was never going to change and it was time to move him on. David Dein was very supportive. We hired a barrister and we didn't think he'd go to prison. Then when he stood in the dock and the judge said, 'I'm going to hand you a custodial sentence,' it was such a shock. To see that kid – by this time he was in his early twenties – handcuffed and being taken away was a nightmare.

Because I was not expecting to go down, all I had was a

toothbrush in my inside pocket. I didn't have a change of clothes or anything, just the suit, shirt and tie that I was wearing. When I was in the van, coming away from court, I was in my suit with a toothbrush in my pocket. If you know you're going to prison, you bring a bag of clothes. But I never really thought that. I brought a toothbrush thinking, 'I guess you never know.' I thought I was being clever. But then, when I got sent down, it didn't sink in for a couple of days. In fact, it took a while to do that.

* * *

Luckily, I was told I would have to serve only six weeks of the three-month sentence. But it's all a bit of a blur. You're taken down into the holding cell in the court, are put into the transport van and then driven to prison. You see those transport vans being driven away from court after the big cases and they are so intimidating inside. It's so tight in there. It's like a cell on wheels. I was thinking, 'I'm going to prison, what's it going to be like? What's going to happen?' I've watched all the films, had all these thoughts, and had no idea what it would really be like. I had so many things going through my head.

I was thinking while I was in that van, 'This better not be like the films. I better not get stabbed, mugged or raped!' I was shitting myself. You watch the films and it looks absolutely horrendous. I didn't have a clue because I'd never seen what the actual inside of a prison looked like, except in the films. I was thinking, 'Will I have to fight someone to show how hard I am?' I was shitting myself but not once did I break down. I was more thinking about what I'd done, and about how, when I got out, I would put my life right.

Then, when you arrive at the prison, the rest of the inmates are waiting for you because they've heard that a footballer is coming in. I don't know how they get to hear about it.

Not once did I cry. I thought I would be a nervous wreck, but I think I dealt with it better because of where I came from, what I'd seen, but actually I had grown out of that in a way. I was living a different life now. I was famous, living in the public eye, a Premier League player; I had changed my life, though not always in a good way. But I was living in a different atmosphere, a different environment.

The funny part was going down for breakfast. I remember going down in my suit and tie! Everyone was in joggers, jeans or a tracksuit. Sometimes you get given prison clothes with grey bottoms and a white T-shirt or tank top, and yet here I was in a suit, a tie – the works. I'd been so convinced that I wouldn't be sent down to prison that I wouldn't need anything else. I did get given some trackie bottoms and things to change into. They were probably thinking, 'Is he someone's lawyer – or what?' But, at this point, there I was in a suit.

There are no bars on the doors of the cells. There's a big heavy door slamming with a little shutter that they peep through to make sure you've not hung yourself. You have a toilet in there, a TV, a radio – if you've brought a radio. It's not as bad as you would imagine. I would not wish anyone to go in there, because the biggest issue is the boredom. It's as boring as shit. It's not even like being locked in your house. You're locked in a room. There's only so much TV you can watch.

It was a Category A prison and I was supposed to be in a Category B because I'm not seen as a danger to society. The Category A is tough, but it's not what you expect. It's modern, all split up into wings, the prisoners on drugs and guns charges in one, those convicted of GBH in another, and then no one mixes with the paedophiles or rapists because these people would get killed or battered for their horrible crimes. However, all prisoners, when they first arrive, are put on the House Wing, so, at that stage, you may not know what anyone else has done.

Then you've got D Wing for terrorists and they get given differently colour uniform: it's multicoloured.

You get checked into House Wing and that's where you get allocated a cell, get put into the right part of the prison for why you're in there. When I was checked in, I didn't have a clue. I was actually asked if I wanted to share a cell. I asked to be on my own, because you just don't know who you'll end up with! But the boredom is the worst thing and, if I had my time again, I'd definitely share.

It was the Woodhill prison in Aylesbury. It's not crazy, it is quite relaxed. But I'd been told I'd be sent to a Category B prison, so they kept telling me I'd be transferred. Two days passed, then five days, and still nothing. I kept saying, 'Guv, when am I being transferred?' Everyone calls the governor 'Guv'. I kept asking what was happening, then, a few days later, there's a knock on the door and it's the guv'nor saying I was being made to stay in the Category A. It was all because of the attention that I would bring, the photographers hanging around. I would be a risk and yet I was thinking, 'That's not my fault.' I was thinking it was unfair.

They promised to protect me more – great! You just don't get prisoners for drink-driving offence in Category A prisons. They promised to keep my door open and things like that but, nonetheless, I was stuck in a Category A even though I wasn't locked up in my cell the whole time. They also let me shower on my own. I've got to admit that I was nervous about that! I asked if I could and they let me, because you hear all the stories from the films. There was no way I was putting myself in that position. They did give me some special treatment like that.

I remember playing table tennis against a guy for about an hour or so. He was a good player. It was when I first arrived and was still in the House Wing. We were chatting away, having banter, and later on I figured out that he'd raped someone. He had been locked off with the rapists and paedophiles and they weren't normally allowed to mix with the other prisoners. When I was waiting to go to the gym with the rest of the inmates, I saw the fella again. I started asking questions and someone told me, 'He's raped someone.'

MENTAL

You think to yourself, 'I was playing table tennis with him!' I found that really difficult to take in. He seemed OK, but then to hear that really shocked me.

But, as I've said, when you're in the House Wing you really don't know what anyone has done. The reason everyone is put there to start with is that there are more guards there than anywhere else. They wanted to keep me there so they could watch me at all times, because I could have been a bit of a target.

I didn't get any hassle at all. I was in the papers for one week solid. It was a huge story. I had so many people coming up to me, even guards saying, 'Can you sign this for me?' Then inmates coming up to my door and saying, 'Have you got a smoke.' No, I don't smoke. 'You don't smoke? Oh, OK, can you sign this?' The thing is that everyone knew I was coming there before I even got there. The whole prison knew I was coming. When I went to the gym I could see people saying, 'There's that Pennant guy.'

We did have a football team and there were regular games against the young offenders. I played only once and that was enough! They were running about, so rough, going for the ball like you wouldn't believe. They were going in for tackles and I was thinking, 'Jesus! I can't believe this.' It was absolute madness. We played on a horrible Astroturf. It was just like carpet. When you slide, half your skin comes off. They didn't give a shit. They were sliding, diving in, absolutely out of control. One time

I had the ball and was running through, thinking, 'This is a piece of piss.' Then someone came flying in. I thought he was Superman! He came from nowhere! I jumped out of the way like you would never believe. It was like I were in the Olympics! I was getting out in two weeks and this guy was trying to take me out and put me out for a year! It was like something out of *Mean Machine*, that film with Vinnie Jones about a prison football team. I didn't see a referee. I don't think there was one, it was a free-for-all. It was crazy. There were young guys as well, aged twenty, twenty-one. I played with the young offenders. They were as fit as anything and some of them wanted to make a name for themselves. 'I did him, I took Pennant out.' That sort of thing. So I decided that I would just stick to the gym from then on!

You were allowed to go to the gym once a week but Birmingham City spoke to the prison and they organised it so I could go in every day, morning and afternoon. I was bulking up so my muscles wouldn't waste away from not working at all, and I would be in good shape when I came out. I got a little bit of special treatment with these regular gym visits, which was nice.

But, as we've seen, the biggest thing was boredom. That's my biggest memory. I don't know how on earth some people do sixteen years in there. It's scary when you're not used to that environment. For someone like me, it was very difficult.

You get given jobs, cleaning up, mopping the floors,

cleaning up your cell, preparing bed sheets, all sorts of things. There was quite a lot of work to be done. You could also read books and I got so many letters from all sorts of people. I got so much fan mail. Girls sent me letters, knickers, pictures, the lot. It was a bit crazy. The guards must have seen a few things! They probably got a right eyeful.

The thing is that, because you're so bored, you write back. I was asking for a few more pictures! By the end, I had a whole big bag of stuff – clothes, underwear, all sorts of stuff that girls had sent me.

I got kind of friendly with a few people, including some of the workers there, and people would want to talk about football, come for an autograph and so on.

* * *

Eventually, it was time for getting out. Sky picked me up. The first thing I said to him was, 'Get me a McDonald's.' He was fuming with me because there was press everywhere following us, taking pictures. 'You get out of prison, the first thing you do is get a McDonald's. You're a professional footballer!' I was telling him they wouldn't see me in the back of the car. He was livid. He called me a disgrace, an absolute disgrace. But he still got me one! I had a Big Mac, big fries and a milkshake. It was great; it was fantastic! I couldn't wait to get out, have a McDonald's and get laid! I was desperate to nick a bird. It was a good feeling.

SKY ANDREW: The first thing he wanted to do was go to McDonald's and there he is in McDonald's signing autographs. I told him to stop signing autographs because he wasn't a celebrity. He said to me: 'You're not my security, you're my agent.' I was trying to protect him and him with money and fame was an absolute nightmare. He was an absolute nightmare!

But I still had to wear a tag because they'd released me early. So I was playing in the Premier League with that tag! I was put under house arrest, then the tag was put on and usually you're in your house from 7 p.m. to 7 a.m., but, because of training and games, they allowed me to be out of the house until midnight, so I could travel back from wherever I had to be at whatever time. That was a bit of a touch, as it meant I could go out with the boys, have a bit of fun, have a few beers, just as long as I was back home by midnight.

I remember more than a few close shaves! A few times my mates were going out, having a big night, and I was thinking I had to be in – but I still managed to say that I would come out for a cheeky one! Then towards the end of my allotted time, I was saying, 'One more drink.' Then, with two minutes till midnight, I was sprinting home to get in before the curfew. If you miss it three times you go back inside and serve the rest of your sentence. But I was playing with fire and I nearly missed the curfew. There was a little bell box at home and you had to be back by midnight. I remember being out with my mates, looking at my watch and thinking, 'I'd better run!' I made it back at 11.59 I've got to admit one night I was thinking, 'This might be worth a strike!' But I ran back and got back just in time.

I played football with the tag when I came out. I think it was just a couple of games, one against Tottenham, and I think we drew. I got a lot of stick from the Spurs fans but the Birmingham supporters were fantastic.

It was funny, really, because a comedian on the telly at the time said, 'Why is he wearing a tag during games? Don't they know there's thirty thousand people watching him!'

KEVIN JAMES: I remember the game for Arsenal when he was hungover and scored the hat-trick. When the team was read out, Jermaine said he was just slumped on in his seat, head between his knees, feeling sick, and then he was told he was playing!

But he'd do that so often. He'd live badly, have nights out, drink and eat the wrong stuff. But then he'd get up the next day and be Man of the Match. He actually set a club record at Birmingham for being voted Man of the Match. He took it off Robbie Savage.

We used to play a lot of computer games, a tennis game; we'd play until really late. I remember going to bed at midnight, then I woke up at 4.30 a.m. or 5 a.m., heard this noise from the lounge and went and had a look. There was Penn, playing this tennis game and saying, 'I'm not going to bed until I beat this guy.' He was playing the computer! Next to him was a pizza box and a big bottle of fizzy drink – and he'd got a game that day. I said to him, 'Are you going to have breakfast?' He just said no, he might have some Lucozade, and ordered a cab. He went off and I thought he was going to be in a terrible state. We both got in that night, him from his game, me from mine, and I said, 'How did it go?' He just replied, 'All right, yeah, I was Man of the Match.' That's the stuff he used to do.

And, no matter what, Steve Bruce loved him. He absolutely loved him. I went to dinner with Jermaine one night and by pure coincidence Brucey was there, and his wife had a real soft spot for him as well. She was always talking to him. They really looked after him and I used to call Brucey his dad. He was a real father figure to him. I'd say to him, 'How's your dad?'

At the time, I had a lot of time to think. I looked back upon my mistakes, things I'd done wrong, and I realised I'd made some bad choices. There I was playing in the Premier League. It was everything I dreamed about as a kid and I was in danger of blowing it.

But Sky said something that really resonated with me. When my back is against the wall, that's when I'm at my best. And at that point in my career I really needed to show my best at football.

At that point in my life, I either needed to really turn it on or turn into another David Bentley which, to anyone who knows me, was never going to happen.

I had talent, which was going to get me only so far because my mentality also had to be right. I've had issues and problems along the way, but it was during that time that I realised what was at stake and that I had to fight for my career.

Steve Bruce was fantastic for me during that time. He even lent me his own flat in Solihull, free of charge, a place to live, three bedrooms. It was out of the way, out of town, and he was trying to make me comfortable. My girlfriend of the time was there as well. It was an incredible gesture.

Without doubt, Steve Bruce was the best manager that I had. He knew I was a little scallywag. He knew I was a bit of a shit. But he also knew that, when I was on the pitch, when I was on his team, I was the best player and that I would deliver. Nine times out of ten I would give a good performance for Steve Bruce. Even though I'd give him problems, I would continue to play and he'd get the best out of me. That was why I played so well for him. I knew he had faith in me. I knew he would play me and put me in the team and I would always set out to repay him by giving everything. I could feel his confidence in me. If I'm a manager then I'm playing my best players. If a player misbehaves and gives problems, then by all means take him aside. But it's what he does on the pitch that is most important. No one needs a manager behaving like a school teacher, not playing someone, losing games and then losing their job rather than getting three points by speaking to the kid, being a parent, giving him a chance. Tell him off, fine him, do whatever, but don't bite off your nose to spite your face. There's no point.

Yeah, I got fined, shouted at, got done, but, ultimately, he would play me. I felt at ease around him. I knew I could say what I wanted around him. He was very approachable. Even when I left Birmingham, we parted on good terms. I probably turned him grey and he put on a few extra pounds of weight as a result of my playing him up, but we never had a row that would end our relationship. I gave him some headaches. But there was never any disrespect on my part towards him. I never told him to fuck off. I think he was probably happy for me to go to Liverpool, because I'd bettered myself and made the most of my talent. If I saw him now, he'd probably say, 'How's it going, bad boy?'

I think he knew what I was like and that's why he took special care of me, especially when I first came out of prison. He sorted out a car for me rather than a taxi. The flat, you see, was in a very quiet area of Solihull, and was nowhere near any shops. I obviously didn't have a car, so it was a ballache.

Brucie made sure that I was looked after. He even got me a driver so, if I needed driving anywhere, he would make sure that I was comfortable. But I've got to be honest: I was bored. It was too quiet for me and I got an apartment in the centre of Birmingham. Steve found out and went mental. 'What the hell are you doing? I've got you a place in a quiet area, and you've moved yourself into the city centre!' He was not happy.

JON FORTUNE: I would get caught in the middle between being a mate with Jermaine and then also trying to keep an eye on him for Sky.

I remember we kept on seeing him driving even when he was banned. So, one day, Sky sent round someone from the office to clamp the car. When he got there, he went to put a clamp on the car and, as he was just about to do it, Jermaine drove right past him in another car!

He rang Jermaine and said, 'What's going on?' Jermaine said, 'Yeah, I'm at the train station, about to get the train to Liverpool.' Then he even did an impression of a Tannoy announcement from a train station: 'The 13.34 is leaving. . .' He'd seen him, caught him red-handed and yet Jermaine was still lying, trying to make up a story. He'd always have an excuse: the ban was over, he'd got a month break or whatever. Any sort of story – he'd always have an angle or an excuse.

The driver was Chris Whyte, the former Arsenal and Leeds player. He was there to pick me up, take me to training and he was there twenty-four/seven. I was asking him every two minutes, 'Chris, can you pick me up?' I guess he was also being asked to keep tabs on me and report back to the club.

But a friend had a party. A few of the boys were asking me to go and I was just thinking it was only a warm-down.

I got a cab there, got a cab back, and it all reached Steve Bruce. I walked in the next day and his face was tomato red, the way he gets when he's absolutely fuming. He was shouting and screaming, 'You fucking stink – I can smell it from here! You were out until three in the morning!'

I said, 'Gaffer, it was only until two! It was a party!' But, not surprisingly, he wasn't impressed. 'You're a disgrace. The fans are furious.'

I told him no one saw me – and then suddenly he said, 'I've got a picture of you!' He showed me a picture of me with two beers in my hands.

'Gaffer, that's not me!' I was trying to explain that I was just holding one for someone but, not surprisingly, he didn't believe me. He was literally pushing me out of the door, pushing me out of the building. You really didn't want to cross him or get on his bad side, because you'd really know about it.

But for the next game I was in the starting line-up and he was so forgiving to me.

Yes, Steve used to call me his 'bad boy' and he used to run a fines system. We all had to pay cash – and I was always having to pay up.

SKY ANDREW: While he was banned, he carried on driving. So, once, I got someone else to text him saying, 'This is the police, we're watching you.' He texted back saying that they couldn't be watching him because he was on the platform at King's Cross station. The lies were happening constantly.

Poor old Chris Whyte – Huggy Bear, we called him – was driven mad. Steve Bruce was so desperate to sign Pennant permanently when he hired Chris Whyte as his driver, security and the man who'd do everything for him. He would give poor old Chris Whyte the runaround. He wouldn't know whether Jermaine was in Birmingham or Manchester. Every day he'd ring me up and say, 'Where's Jermaine?' He could be waiting outside the training ground and he'd still give him the slip to go and see some chicks or go with his mates drinking. I've lost count of the number of times I sat him down and gave him a final warning. Lost count.

I was giving my everything at Birmingham, playing well, scoring goals and I was playing at my best. But, even though we weren't getting results, I was still standing out in the team even when we got relegated.

CHAPTER 6

YOU'LL NEVER WALK ALONE

One of the craziest things that have ever happened to me on a football pitch was being tapped up by Steven Gerrard in the middle of a game. Here was one of my heroes, the captain of Liverpool, the team I grew up supporting as a kid, the team I always wanted to play for, and Gerrard was trying to get the number of my agent during a match!

I was in the middle of the field, near Gerrard, whom I had never even spoken to before, and he said in his thick Scouse accent, 'All right lad, who's your agent?' I was thinking, 'What?' It was crazy. I even said to him, 'Why? Do you know him?' I added, 'Do you need his details? I'll give you his details!'

I grew up as a Liverpool fan and it blew my mind. I had always dreamed of playing for Liverpool and I remember that when I signed for Arsenal, I did an interview and was asked what my dream was. I said it was to play alongside Michael Owen. I'd just signed for Arsenal and they'd got me saying I wished I'd signed for Liverpool!

I wasn't aware that Liverpool were watching me. I was seeing a girl who worked there, and she told me, 'Oh, by the way, Liverpool are watching you, they're always asking for tickets because they want to see you play.' She told me just before we played Liverpool. When we did play them I ran my socks off, playing as well as I could, running until I couldn't run any more.

What can you do? I supported Liverpool as a kid. As soon as I heard of Liverpool's interest and knew that it was real, I was onto my agent the whole time pleading with him to make it happen. 'Sky, is it true? Is it true? You've got to make it happen!' I remember falling out with Sky. We'd just been relegated and I remember saying, 'I'm not speaking to you until you make this happen. Don't even bother calling me until you've sorted it out. Get me a move to this club!'

SKY ANDREW: Everyone saw him as a bit of a risk. How he got to Liverpool was quite amazing, really. Birmingham were obviously prepared to sell him, so I knew I could speak to other clubs. I spoke to Wigan Athletic, and it was Paul Jewell in charge at the time. Wigan turned him down and said he was not for them. Then he went to Liverpool!

It was Rafa Benítez, Rick Parry and Steven Gerrard, who spoke to him on the pitch. Liverpool were all over him. But I'll be honest: people were shocked. The amazing thing was that I knew we were struggling to get another Premier League club. There were stories of his drinking, going out and not being reliable.

Luckily enough for him, he'd played two great games against Liverpool. He played against John Arne Riise and absolutely terrorised him, and played great. That's why they wanted to sign him.

I had to go back to pre-season training with Birmingham. Nothing had happened, we'd just been relegated and suddenly I got the call one day. I was just putting on my boots to go out for training. It was Sky. 'Jermaine – where are you? Get your arse on the train to Liverpool. Get dressed, put your clothes on, get on the next train and meet me in Liverpool.' Why? 'They've accepted a bid from Liverpool.'

FORMER LIVERPOOL CHIEF EXECUTIVE RICK PARRY: We had been negotiating for weeks on Dani Alves. It was a big fee: we agreed €17 million. It would have been a good signing for us, but suddenly Rafa got cold feet and wanted to go for Jermaine Pennant and a striker instead. It wasn't either or. But, like a lot of managers, Rafa could see that, for the same money as Alves, he could sign two, possibly even three players.

I have never been so happy in my life. A few weeks before that I was so angry: we'd been relegated; I'd played so well; no one had come in; and then, suddenly, everything came together.

The only team who had come in that summer had been Everton. I remember Sky telling me that, if I went to Everton, I could never, ever go to Liverpool. 'OK, I won't go to Everton, then.' It really was as simple as that.

I had always wanted to play for Liverpool. I had played against Everton in the Carling Cup when I was at Arsenal and I had just ripped them to bits and we won 3–1. We put out a young team, including me, and they had a full-strength team. And we still won! That's why Everton wanted me and why David Moyes tried to sign me.

SKY ANDREW: I've tried really hard to do everything correctly. Arsenal agreed a fee with Everton for about £4.5 million. David Dein said it'd be agreed. They gave us permission to speak to Everton and we spoke to Bill Kenwright and David Moyes. They wanted him. I spoke to Jermaine and, nine times out of ten, if a big club comes in, your club agrees a fee then you're off. I asked him, 'Do you want to do it?' He wasn't sure. I told him that, if he signed for Everton, he could never sign for Liverpool. He asked me, 'Why? It's just another football club.'

We had another conversation about what he wanted in his career. It was a difficult conversation, because he was not on big money. Everton would have meant a huge increase in his money and he would have been starting for a big club; and yet, in the end, I warned him that, as a Liverpool supporter, he'd have little chance to sign for them if he went to Everton. He thought about it, rang me back and didn't want to do it.

It's a tricky one and we were subsequently proved right. Everton's a great club and I've got a lot of respect for David Moyes. But, for Jermaine, I didn't want for him to turn round to me at the end of his career and have regrets about not playing for Liverpool.

There was no way I was going to Everton, because Liverpool were my boyhood club. I had Robbie Fowler on my shirt. I watched John Barnes. And, as a kid, all I wanted to do was sign for Liverpool.

When it happened, I was just so excited. I remember running out of the dressing room at Birmingham, barely got changed, and I was shouting, 'See you later, lads.' I remember telling them all that I was off to sign for Liverpool, and David Dunn just said, 'You fucking bastard!'

It was a strange time, because I thought I'd done well at Birmingham, played really well, and yet no one had come in. Obviously it's because of my history. There was no guarantee a big club would come in for me. I'd just been relegated from the Premier League and I didn't know what would happen next. But I was so shocked when Sky pulled it off and set up the deal. It was always the dream for me to sign for Liverpool.

Sky showed them that I had changed, I had grown up, and yet I was like the little boy again. It was a dream to play for Liverpool and it's all I ever wanted.

I remember actually saying to Robbie Fowler, who was there at the time, 'I used to wear your jersey as a little kid.' It was a dream come true.

I signed for Liverpool in July 2006 for £6.7 million and it remains one of the best days of my life, certainly the best day of my career. It was incredible.

GARY PENNANT: I should have been more of a dad for him. We would speak every so often, but it wasn't until he went to Birmingham that I saw more of him. When he went to Leeds and Watford, my brother Mark went and watched him every week. He always had someone there, his uncle or his auntie. Obviously, it was his dad who he probably needed.

It was when he was at Birmingham that I began to sort myself out. I started going every week and we got a lot closer and I think he was happier then. I think it showed as well because he played really well, well enough for him to get a move to Liverpool.

I'm a Liverpool fan. It's the same for me, my brother and Jermaine. We were all Liverpool fanatics. I was over the moon when he signed for Liverpool. It was great.

The first thing Rafa Benítez did when I signed was to say to me, 'I want you to write down all the negative stuff that surrounds you.' It was like a brainstorm. I remember putting down the first thing: going out. Why do you go out? Girls. He got me to put everything down: crap friends, crap lifestyle and crap around me. He did the same thing with Craig Bellamy when he signed, because he, like me, had a bit of a past. That was obviously something he does regularly.

Rafa Benítez is a brilliant tactician. He knows when to make substitutions, what to do to win games, how to set up teams – and he's spot on.

But all the time, in the background, I was so worried that my past would catch up with me and ruin everything for me at Liverpool. Sure enough, it did. Just when everything seemed to be going right, my dad was caught in a newspaper sting, trying to sell drugs to an undercover reporter.

It made front-page news. He ended up going to prison again and, once more, things had come back to haunt me. My dad was filmed by the *News of the World*, taking the reporter into the den, doing a drugs deal, and it did make me feel embarrassed.

It was the reason why I pushed myself away: I just knew that one day the truth would come out. I didn't want it to affect me or make it difficult for my career.

It was one of the reasons why I didn't have much of a relationship with my father. I didn't want to be linked to drugs and that sort of scene. When it did come out, I hoped it was in a newspaper, meaning it would disappear the next day; and yet it was always difficult.

To a certain extent, I brought myself up to deal with emotions alone. I just dealt with things myself, tried to block things out, tried not to show any emotion and not to let things get to me. I did it the best I could.

It made it worse by my trying to bottle things up, without doubt. There's a lot of stuff that I bottled up through my family, a lot of issues and anything to do with emotion. I had no one to turn to, no one to talk it through with. Most kids have a mum or a dad to talk things through and say, 'Mum, this has happened. Can you help?' I had none of that.

If you bottle it up, you *build* it up, make it worse, and it really affects you and you probably don't learn from your mistakes. That's certainly been the case with me.

I would say the only person I could turn to later was my agent, Sky Andrew. We would talk all the time. He knew what sort of player he had on his books, he wanted to invest a lot of time and effort in me and, at the same time, we sort of formed a bond. We had a father–son relationship. It's why we're still together now. He worked his socks off to get me the best deals, best contracts and best clubs. Depending on how much trouble I was in, he would try to bail me out and, like a father, would, try to help me, would talk things through.

I found that a very difficult time. It also came amid a very exciting time in my life and in my career with Liverpool.

SKY ANDREW: Because of the way he grew up, a lot of him is to do with not knowing what's right or wrong or what's true or not. In the early days, I saw the signs when we had a night out with one of his first girlfriends. He couldn't drive but went on and on about wanting a car. Eventually, I bought him an Audi A4. Because he didn't have a license, he could only drive when he was in the car with someone who did. So, on his eighteenth birthday, we went to a restaurant in London, he, my girlfriend and I, and his girlfriend. I ordered some drinks and said, 'Jermaine, congratulations on your eighteenth birthday.' Then the girl looked at me in horror, burst out crying and ran to the toilets. My girlfriend chased after her and I said to Jermaine, 'What's going on?' It turns out that he had told her that he was twenty. He'd kept stringing her along by saying that he didn't want to drive. Could she? And that was the beginning of his tall stories.

Those sorts of tales started when people told him that his mum was dead. Then when he found out she wasn't dead. . . Someone called me and said that she was alive. It was so weird. Him being told that wasn't great because it was almost as if he thought it was OK to tell half-truths even with the most important things and subsequently he would make up any old cock-and-bull story to get himself out of trouble.

All through his life, driving and drink was a major issue. If he had never drunk, never stepped into a car, then he would have been a great player – not just a *good* player, but a truly *great* player. But drinking and driving was the worst of all his problems. He always wanted to live on the edge. Every time he got banned he just carried on driving and carried on buying cars. He got banned and went and bought himself an Aston Martin.

I had everybody in the UK on Pennant watch. If he went in to buy a car then they would phone me. Jermaine was so arrogant with it all. Then he would phone me, start having a go at me, saying it's his money, his car, and if he wants to buy a car then it's his decision. While he was banned, he bought an Aston Martin and wrapped it up in chrome.

Another time he was banned, he drove a Ferrari into Liverpool's training ground and was signing autographs. It was put it on YouTube and someone called me and told me what had happened. I said, 'He can't be doing that because he's banned. It can't be him.' Then I went on YouTube and saw it for myself. He used to drive to the Arsenal training ground for a year-and-a-half while banned before I found out what he was doing. He parked in the car park at the back, and then walked in. He did that for about six months.

Liverpool was a brilliant experience. To play in front of the Kop was amazing. My first ever game at Anfield was a Champions League qualifier against Maccabi Haifa. I got Man of the Match. I can remember having to go to the Carlsberg lounge afterwards, being asked questions by so many Scousers. I was so proud, and it was a great moment.

It was a dream from my boyhood, and the people around me really helped me to settle in straightaway. I was just dying to get the first game under way because I'd had a good pre-season and couldn't wait to get started.

MENTAL

Liverpool is such a huge club and you don't realise just *how* huge until you play for them, see the fans, play at Anfield, soak up the atmosphere. It was a dream for me. The fan base was massive, no matter what country I was in. We went away in pre-season, played in Europe, and the fans were incredible. I could instantly tell it was going to be a big challenge.

But it was so good to play in nearly every game. Every single time they sang my name, the hairs on the back of my neck stood up. It was an incredible experience.

When I was walking through the tunnel I saw Steven Gerrard touch the 'This is Anfield' sign, but I deliberately didn't, out of respect. I didn't think I'd earned the right, not when so many greats had ritually done so before me. And I'd done nothing yet. Down the years, I'd seen so many great players, my heroes, go out of the tunnel, the fans singing 'You'll Never Walk Alone'.

That first match was a nice night, too, not too cold. It was perfect. During the first ten to fifteen minutes, I was so nervous. I didn't want to do too much because I know that, when you play for a big club, you get judged very quickly, and it's just not worth it. You want your first couple of games to start well so the fans warm to you. I wanted to play safe.

So during those first five or ten minutes, I was steady. I played well and made a pass across the box to Craig Bellamy, but it got intercepted and they went down the other end and scored. And I was thinking, 'Oh, my, oh, my.' My heart went plop into my stomach. But then I set up Bellamy again for a goal and we ended up winning the game 2–1. It was a fantastic result for us.

In the second leg I set up Peter Crouch and we went through into the Champions League proper. If we'd lost that, we'd have gone into the Europa League. Wow! What a pressurised start to my Liverpool career! But it really couldn't have gone any better. The Liverpool fans really warmed to me quickly, and I had a nice rapport with them.

There were some good teammates, including Peter Crouch. We always had such a laugh. Steve Finnan was there, too – he was a cool guy.

Stevie G and Jamie Carragher kept themselves to themselves, really. They were the main guys around the place but didn't really get too close to the likes of me in training or match days. We had good banter and stuff but I wasn't particularly close to either of them.

KEVIN JAMES: I remember going up to Liverpool for a day out with Jermaine and the Liverpool players for paintballing. Jermaine had gone online and bought up a load of paintball guns.

I got to the gates of the place and they were covered in paint and there was Jermaine pointing his guns. He was taking it so seriously. It was typical Jermaine!

MENTAL

It was a good city, Liverpool. We had a lot of fun. We got tickets to go to the MTV Europe awards and Gerrard asked the manager to allow us to go. So Rafa sorted out a coach to take us and bring us back. We were supposed to be back by 11.30 p.m. I think I got my own bus home at four in the morning! We ended up having a load of girls back at my house for a party. I had converted my garage into a nightclub. It had everything. I called it 'The Players' Lounge'. It had a bar, DJ booth, chairs, lights, speakers — the works.

I remember waking up and it was carnage. Then I thought, 'Training!' There were girls everywhere, all over the floor, on the bed. It was ridiculous. I panicked, got myself to training, and, as soon as I got there, I was told that I would have to train with the kids.

JON FORTUNE: His converted nightclub in his house at Liverpool. Peter Crouch and his missus were there doing breakdancing and backflips. I gave Crouchie a lift home and I've got a picture somewhere with him sitting in the back all hunched up in an Aston Martin because he could barely get his legs in.

It was so funny. It had decks, a bar and dance floor. He even put a toilet in there, so it was just like a nightclub!

I have to admit that I went off the rails in the 2007/08 season. But the year before that, we reached the Champions League final – and that year was probably my best time at Liverpool, certainly in terms of football and performances. I played so well. I was focused, playing really good football. We came so close to being European champions. And I played some of the best football of my career. I had some crazy ups and downs at Liverpool. But my season in the build-up to the Champions League final was one I will never forget.

CHAPTER 7

THE STUFF OF CHAMPIONS

The Champions League final in 2007 was an experience that I will never forget. It was probably the best and worst night of my career. The best, because I was voted Man of the Match and I knew that I'd played well. I really put myself on a different level. How many players can say they were Man of the Match in a European final? Not many. I felt that I was fulfilling my potential. And all my dreams.

It was also the worst experience, because we'd lost the biggest game of my career, the game I had dreamed of playing for Liverpool all of my life. It was difficult to take but, to be completely honest, I was really happy – even though we ended up losing to AC Milan in a repeat of the final in Istanbul, when Liverpool had won so dramatically on penalties two years earlier.

MENTAL

Everyone still talks about the 'miracle of Istanbul' and how Liverpool came from 3–0 down against one of the great teams of Europe. The incredible fightback, the penalties – it was almost as if people just expected us to turn up and win again. That's what happens to Liverpool – they win European trophies. They had won their fifth in 2005 and now, having reached the Champions League final in 2007, we were expected to win another in Athens.

We did have a good team: a great midfield – Steven Gerrard, Xabi Alonso and Javier Mascherano – and Pepe Reina in goal and Jamie Carragher at the back.

But it really did come on the back of a very strange season. We could have gone out in the qualifying round because we only squeezed through 3–2 on aggregate to Maccabi Haifa. But, from then on, we went from strength to strength.

I produced some of my best performances in the Champions League. But it was a strange season because we had so many unpredictable results, and yet, throughout our inconsistent league form, we were at our best in Europe.

If you look at the results, we seemed to do well against the good teams, and against the lower teams we seemed to struggle. But that seems to be Liverpool's issue. We always appeared to struggle against the teams we should have beaten. It's crazy; it's almost like a curse. It's carried on in more recent seasons for the club.

Through the rounds in Europe, the games in the group stage were a bit hit-and-miss, but we cruised through against Galatasaray, Bordeaux and PSV Eindhoven to win the group.

It is very different in the Champions League group stage from how it is in the knockout because, in the league competition, there are still games to play, but in the knockout one bad result can put you out.

That's why Anfield is so important for Liverpool and has been down the years. It's still the case now: the atmosphere is special – particularly on Champions League days and big European nights – and it gives you such a boost. It's almost a different atmosphere and feeling from the Kop on European nights. They feel the history; they have the expectation and it really lifts the mood. With that feeling of 'one bad result and you're out', it really helps. The atmosphere is just totally different. You just can't replicate that and it's such a big thing, especially when you are playing at home.

I remember playing against Barcelona that season. It was so special. Every game was great to be in. I think realistically we knew we were outside contenders for the UK league – we ended up finishing third and twenty-one points short of Manchester United, who won the title – so our main objective was really to go for the Champions League, and to be part of it was fantastic.

I can remember some of the games so clearly, including a semifinal against Chelsea that we won on penalties after winning the return leg at our place.

Another special game was against Barcelona in the first

knockout stage. To draw them so early is pretty unlucky and, even though they hadn't reached their peak, they had won the trophy in 2006 after beating Arsenal and had Lionel Messi, Xavi and Ronaldinho, who all played against us.

But that game in the Nou Camp will be remembered for one thing in particular: Craig Bellamy's goal celebration.

Craig was a real live wire, a proud Welshman, always loud, aggressive and very determined. I think he actually calmed down a bit while he was at Liverpool, but he was a great player to have on your side.

I just wish I could remember all the stories, but the most memorable one was when he hit John Arne Riise with a golf club and then celebrated with a golf swing. It all happened when we were doing some warm-weather training before the Barcelona game. We had been training hard and we were all saying, 'Let's go out for a bit.' So we all did. I think it was organised for the lads, to be fair, because they put on a little coach for us. We went out to a karaoke bar. Everyone was getting up, doing a bit, singing their songs. They didn't have my kind of music or songs, so I got out of it. Stevie G and Carra sang some songs. We all said to Craig, or 'Bellers', 'Go on, mate. Get up there!' We were egging him on. But he just kept saying, 'I can't be arsed.' And then Riise was getting on his back – obviously, he'd had a couple of drinks. 'Get up there, get up there.'

Bellers was just saying: 'Just fuck off, I'm not interested, I can't be arsed, not tonight.'

And then Riise was egging him on. 'Go on, Bellers, get up there.' Riise was getting more than a bit lairy. 'Ah, you're a shithouse, Craig. You're on tour. You're supposed to be the hard man.'

We were all drinking our beers, thinking, 'Oh-oh! Oh-oh!' It kept going on. Bellers was going, 'You carry on, just carry on. Keep on fucking singing your song. You carry on.'

Eventually, it ended and we all got back to the hotel we were staying at. We'd all gone to our rooms. Crouchie and I went to the injury room, playing a bit of music, having a laugh – though we were told to turn it down, so we did so and went back to our room. Then Steve Finnan came round to the room shouting, 'Fucking hell! You lot – guess what!' We asked, 'What's going on?' Panting, Finnan said, 'Bellamy's just battered Riise with a seven iron!' What the fuck!

Finnan explained that Bellers had a seven iron in his hand. He'd knocked on the door and had been let in. And then he'd gone over to John, who was just lying on the bed. He started saying, 'It was just a joke, Craig! I didn't mean it, I swear! I'm sorry! I'm sorry!'

Bellers screamed at him, 'Say that again. Go on, say it.'

Riise said no – and then Bellers just started whacking him. He hit him a few times. He had his legs up, so took it mainly on the side of his thigh. 'I'm sorry, I'm sorry!' he was screaming. Someone must've told the boss, Rafa Benítez, because he then came round fuming, telling people to get to their rooms. Then, ten minutes after we'd been told to go to our rooms, I crept out to see what was going on – and got caught by the boss, who went mad. And, as always, I copped it!

I came walking out and the boss demanded, 'Why is it always you? Why are you always around, always around, and not where you should be?' I didn't say anything. 'Why you always around? Why you always here?' he kept saying in his Spanish accent. I wanted to crack up, but I couldn't.

I was opposite my room, so took two steps back and was soon inside. Crouchie and I were absolutely pissing ourselves. It was so funny!

That drama was just typical Bellers. Craig has always got something to say for himself! I've played with a few live wires down the years. I played with Joey Barton a few times for the under-twenty-ones. He was a bit of a live wire. But Craig Bellamy is probably the liveliest. He's a right loudmouth. But, actually, he's a lovely guy. When people think about Craig Bellamy, they probably say the same about me: 'Oh, Craig Bellamy, what a prick, what an dickhead!' On the pitch, he is a menace. Always winding people up. But he's a cool guy underneath all that.

I can remember another incident with Bellers. We were playing for Liverpool against Wigan and he was up against Fitz Hall, one of the centre-backs, who is about six foot two. They were having some argy-bargy. Craig was offering him out! Next thing I knew, they were going at it at half-time in the tunnel. I remember saying, 'Craig – he's going to eat you, mate!' Anyway, he survived and they carried on. But when the final whistle went, Craig was straight off the pitch and back into the changing room. Sometimes he says more than he probably should!

I would say Craig Bellamy was also up there as the funniest guy I've played with. But Crouchie is another really funny guy from my time at Liverpool and then later at Stoke City. Crouchie is a prankster, but sly with it. He would come out with jokes, practical jokes and little comments, and then try and make himself look quiet and innocent. Also, he is so tall, and always reckoned he had great dance moves. So we'd say to him 'Go on, Crouchie, show us your snake hips.' Then he'd do this salsa thing with his hips, a circular motion, some sort of number eight with his long skinny body, trying to dance. He's a very funny guy. Also he is so tall, and always reckoned he had great dance moves. So we'd say to him, 'Go on, Crouchie, show us your snake hips.' Then he'd be doing this salsa thing with his hips, a circular motion, some sort of number eight with his long skinny body, trying to dance.

Liverpool did try to keep the incident with the golf clubs quiet. In training the next day the matter was brought up on the training field before our session began. Rafa said, 'Whatever has happened, we keep it in house, you know. Are you two fine?' And then he said, 'Riise let me see your leg.' Riise lifted up his leg and it was just blue! Blue and purple! Rafa then said, 'Look, is it sorted?' And they both looked at him and said yeah, then they shook hands. It was bit salty after that, for sure!

Riise didn't train fully for a few days because of it, but still played. Then it came out in the newspapers. When Bellers scored, he took a golf swing by way of celebration. I think that was a bit harsh – and I don't think I saw Riise celebrate with him!

* * *

We beat Barcelona over two legs, which was a fantastic achievement at the time. Barcelona had a fantastic team, including Lionel Messi, Xavi, Andrés Iniesta and Samuel Eto'o. But we did a great job on them. Then we knocked out PSV Eindhoven and got Chelsea in the semifinal again, a rematch of the semifinal of two years earlier, when Liverpool had beaten José Mourinho on the way to winning the trophy in Istanbul.

The games were huge. An all-English semifinal, Benítez v. Mourinho, and the whole Chelsea thing – it was all simply massive. To be honest, the pressure felt as great as if it had been a final. I felt the same pressure going into the semifinals as I did the final.

I had a slight groin strain in the second game at Anfield, so I came off with about ten minutes to go. I had a good game, though. Then it went to penalties. I remember not watching ours, but watching theirs. I couldn't take one, as I'd been substituted. After we won, I tried to run on and celebrate. But that made the groin even worse! I was thinking, 'Oh, fuck, I'm gonna be injured now – and miss the final!' I actually thought that would be the case, so there I was, hobbling over to the lads, clapping, hobbling back up, making my groin work, trying to celebrate.

It was also a strange feeling having played against Ashley Cole, because he is such a good mate and yet was always so tough as a full-back. Obviously, we'd trained together for four or five years and he knew my strengths, and he knew how I didn't like it when you get closed down real quick. He always leaves one on you as well! Never mind that we're mates. It was always tough, but that's how football is, it's not meant to be easy.

But, once we'd reached the final, there was no way I was going to miss it. It was in Athens and the build-up was so exciting. It felt incredible to be part of such a game.

You start buzzing from the moment you get your European tracksuit on – the Champions League logo, the achievement of just reaching the final. It's all so big. You start the build-up with training, and even that's special because the tactics for a European game are often different. With each day and each training session, it becomes more tense, and suddenly you're picturing the final in your head. With every day it builds, and suddenly you're watching this hype on Sky Sports and you go to bed trying to sleep while thinking that you're about to play the biggest game of your life.

I kept asking myself, 'Am I going to have a good game? Are we going to win it? What can I do?' You talk yourself through your own game plan. But no matter how much you think about it, and even if you set yourself up with a mini game plan, that goes out of the window when you cross that white line.

So you have to make sure you get a good sleep in the hotel the night before. And then, as soon as you wake up, it's all about preparation – from the minute you open your eyes until you cross that white line.

Preparation – it's largely about rituals. Little things. I had a shave before, for instance – I wanted to feel clean and fresh. Then there's doing your hair so it looks all right. I don't really have any other pre-match rituals, and no superstitions.

The other thing in the build-up to that game was the amount of preparation that Rafa Benítez put in. People talk about him as a great tactician, one of the best at setting up teams to win one-off games. And I'd agree with that. He's incredible, an amazingly well-prepared coach, particularly for European games. If there's one manager you believe can get a result, it's Rafa. He goes into minute detail. He points out the strengths and weaknesses of the opposition.

We were underdogs against Barcelona and probably underdogs against AC Milan, our opponents in the final, and so it was definitely about how we should set up, and how we should close down opponents.

But, if you're favourites, you probably concentrate more on your own game, because you believe you can go out, and, if you play to your strengths and to your best, you win.

However, the underdogs still need to have a plan, to try

to close down the opposition. And I think that's what Rafa really enjoyed. Setting up a team and a tactical plan. It got us through against Barcelona – and AC Milan was up next.

Often Rafa would change the team completely, play with one upfront or something, to try to stop the opposition and put more in midfield, which has since become a standard tactic in the game. Every player would know his job, have it drilled into him. They'd all know whom they were up against, know how to close a player down, know which way a player turns, and so on. You watch it on video so many times that it's drummed into you.

Rafa would study the opposition so carefully, and then set out to disrupt and counteract them. For example, in the 2005 final, when Liverpool beat AC Milan in Istanbul, Rafa surprised everyone by picking Harry Kewell in the starting line-up. He came off early and it didn't really work, but that just goes to show that he will pull off a surprise to try to win a game. In our line-up, we had a strong XI. There wasn't a big surprise, but we were kept guessing.

That's the thing with Rafa: he is a real tactician and I think he enjoys that reputation. He likes to be seen as clever with his tactics, his substitutions, and I'm still trying to work out if he's a tactical genius or he's just got lucky with some of his decisions.

You can see through games when you watch him on Sky Sports now – he still does that. Sometimes it looks as if he's hardly looking at the game. He's always looking at his little notepad, writing down details and notes as if he were going on for a test at half time. He then takes you through his notes in the dressing room, makes a point of outlining what needs addressing, and on the board he will start using bits and bobs and giving instructions and telling each player what's wrong or right or what he wants more or less of. If anything needs changing, if someone's on fire, then he'll leave them. But, if he thinks something needs changing, he won't hesitate.

Every day we would have meetings and we were staying in a top-notch hotel. The food was nice, because that's important. It was a nice atmosphere around the whole place. Everyone bought into the preparation, was very focused and very serious.

After the final was the time you could relax, have some downtime, enjoy time with friends and family, go on holiday with the boys and all that. But, before that, you've got a massive task in hand. You've had a long season but are ready to give it one last effort.

Each evening, we would chill in people's rooms, trying not to think too much of the game because obviously you don't want it taking over, making you too nervous to the extent that it starts affecting your performance. So you have to get a good balance between hard work and a bit of banter around the hotel.

By the time we got to the hotel in Athens, the whole city was taken over by the build-up to the game and there were loads of fans hanging around the hotel. They catch wind straightaway where you're staying, so we don't go out into the lobby much because of the sheer number of supporters down there, many taking pictures. It's lucky when you've got Steven Gerrard, though, because he takes every bit of limelight! From the time you get off the coach, you're sweating, you just want to shower and you've got hundreds of people saying, 'Can I have a picture, can I have a photo?' But it's ten times more for Stevie. So, on getting off the coach, I'd try to hide behind him, then head straight to my room, looking back as I did so to see that he was still signing away.

We'd done some warm-weather training in Portugal, so that prepared us for the heat in Athens and it was warming up considerably because, by then, it was May.

We also had a lot of experience and incredible players. Gerrard, Alonso, Jamie Carragher and Fernando Torres. He came after the first final and he was an incredible player, such a good finisher. Then we had Dirk Kuyt, who was such a hard worker. Being brutally honest, I'd say he was probably bang average, didn't have great pace or skill, and yet he ran and ran. He would work his socks off, was a good lad, and would get in the team for his work rate.

After all the build-up came Rafa's biggest moment, which was the pre-match team talk at the hotel. He mentioned the previous final, when we beat them. That would've been the main basis for trying to give us confidence. We talked about their strengths and we knew they were very good. But Rafa told us not to be worried if they scored. If they score two, don't worry. If they scored three, don't worry.

MENTAL

We'd done it before, coming back from 3–0 down, and, if that was what it would take, we would do it again. He warned us that they would be so up for it, motivated by revenge and determined. It was stuff like that. He would say how good we were, reminding us that you don't get to a final by luck. You earn it. You earn it over two games in the semifinal and right through the round. So he was putting the belief back in us. When we went out there, he told us, we'd got a chance, just as they had, even if they were favourites again.

Rafa was known for his tactics, but it was a good speech, one to really lift the players. It's a huge occasion even as you walk out with the ceremony, the players lining up and the trophy on the pitch in front of you.

And I can remember going out there before the game, Steven Gerrard having advised against touching the trophy. When you walk out there, it's in the middle and you walk past it as you line up before kick-off. Gerrard had said in the changing rooms, 'Nobody touch the trophy as they walk past it! Do not touch it! They did it in Istanbul. I can remember seeing Maldini and a few others touch it. They touched it and we won it.' It was on superstition, I guess. Or maybe about thinking it was theirs already. But, whatever reason, he just kept saying, 'Nobody touch it.' And, funnily enough, none of *their* players touched it as we walked past. I remember looking and thinking, 'Let's see if anyone touches it.' But no one did!

It's funny because, even if there's no truth in it, it still plays on your mind. You don't need anything going against you when you're playing in the final. That one-game final!

Then the strangest thing happened to me before the game – and it could probably happen only to me! I'd got three or four tickets for my family – my dad, an uncle and so on. When you're a player, you get given tickets and then you put them in an envelope, put the names on the envelope and give it to the representative who deals with the tickets and families. They then take them to the ticket office or whatever. So I'd done my normal stuff, left the tickets to be picked up, and thought nothing more of it.

Then, towards the end of the first half, there was a Tannoy announcement, which was really loud on the pitch: 'Jermaine Pennant, can you please go to the ticket office.' Yeah, sure, no problem! I'm in a Champions League final. Let me just tell the ref I'll be back in a minute; let me pop up and sort this out! Obviously, I'm joking, but I heard the announcement and there I am on the pitch. It was the strangest thing! It was like one of those announcements getting someone in the crowd to move their car. But this was to me – and I was playing on the pitch!

I don't know if they thought it was someone else in the stand called Jermaine Pennant or actually believed it was me. I could see everybody looking around on the pitch at me and I couldn't believe it! I didn't know what to think or what the hell was going on. But I just had to banish it from my mind and get on with it.

After the game I looked at my phone and my uncle

had obviously been absolutely raging. And I asked him what happened. He said there were no tickets. So what had happened was that I'd left them and, Scousers being Scousers, they will do anything to get tickets.

'Jermaine Pennant has left me some tickets,' they would have said. And the ticket office would have just seen tickets left there and probably wouldn't even have asked the person's name. They'd just probably said, 'I am Mr Pennant.' So my uncle had flown over, gone to get the tickets for all of them and there were none there. They even got delayed on the way home! I'd left the tickets as normal. I couldn't physically give them to them because it was impossible. I couldn't leave them at the hotel, either, because they'd flown out on the day of the game and it was too late. But, hey, that's the story of my life. It's never simple!

GARY PENNANT: I remember the Champions League final and the Tannoy message. I heard the Tannoy: 'Can Jermaine Pennant go to the turnstiles to meet your family to give them the tickets.' He was on the pitch!

But, once you cross that white line, despite the huge occasion and the fact that it's a great atmosphere, and once you're getting touches of the ball, it feels like just another game. That's how it was at times. When I had the ball, and I was going past a few players, putting crosses in and playing well, it was easy; it wasn't overwhelming at all. You're expecting, for some reason, the Champions League final to be different in some way. But ultimately, it's a football game. It's the same game you play when you're playing at home, just on a bigger stage, so it's no different. Yes, it's important, but just another game.

So that was how I took it during the final and probably why I played so well. If people read too much into it, then I guess it can take hold of you, get into your head, and you don't want to do certain things because it's such big stage and because of the number of people watching. But none of that crossed my mind – that I was going be watched by people all over the world, as if it were the Champions League final. This is when I'm on the pitch, of course. When I'm off it in the build-up, I do think about this stuff, but when I'm on it and getting the ball, when I'm on my pass doing my duty, none of that even enters my head.

It's like that in every game I play. If you get a good early touch, nice little lay-off, good pass, then you're thinking, 'Ah! It's gonna be a good game today.' Similarly, if you do something bad early on, then it knocks your confidence and it goes wrong.

The first thing I achieve is very important to me, the first couple of touches. Even if it's just a one-two, or something simple. If it's crisp and correct and how it should be, I feel I'll have a good game. I think that's one of my superstitions. That's probably the only one I've got.

I played a one-two with Dirk Kuyt quite early on in

the game. I always see it on pictures and the Milan keeper getting down to his right and saving it. I always think back, 'Why didn't I just rifle it high? If I'd scored, what would I have done?' I'd probably have jumped over the barrier, taken my shirt off or something, and ended up getting booked. Mind you, that would have been worth it!

Among their team were players such as Maldini, Nesta, Pirlo and Kaká. They had a brilliant side. Kaká was fantastic, a real fighter. We tried everything to try to stop him from getting the ball. We had put in place lots of plans to do so, but, as soon as the ball went his way, all the plans went out of the window.

I bet they were looking at me thinking: 'Hmm. Who is Jermaine Pennant?' I think they knew once the game was finished! Massimo Ambrosini was marking me but I gave him a tough time. Everyone had played at the highest level and there I was among them. To get Man of the Match for our team was so pleasing, because you don't get a harder test or game than that.

We would lose the game, but I'd have played well. After about half an hour of the match, the ball was continually coming to me. That happens only when you're the strong outlet. I just felt I had this adrenaline in me; I felt so sharp. I can remember weaving past a few players, putting in balls. I just knew that day was to be *my* day. The pitch was big as well. There was quite a lot of space. And that is my perfect scenario. So, after half an hour, I knew I was playing well in a game to remember.

In the second half, I was just so relaxed and got comfortable. I loved putting in a corner for the goal. It's like the icing on the cake. It was obviously late, and we made it 2–1 with a minute to go, but, even so, there was still belief. You could hear the fans when that goal went in, you could sense they thought another fightback was on. As soon as that goal when in, AC Milan also absolutely shit themselves! They knew what had happened in 2005 – and suddenly . . . We had an attempt as well, very, very late on it. It was Stevie G. He had a chance but he kind of scuffed it.

Afterwards, I came out on the pitch. There's a picture on my Instagram somewhere of me, Harry Kewell, Steven Gerrard and Xabi Alonso, standing there with our socks down, shin pads out, with the runners-up medals round our necks, obviously watching them taking their turn to walk up and get their medals. You could tell by our facial expressions we were all devastated. But, at the same time, I was thinking, 'I played in a Champions League final.' There was this feeling inside, something about what I'd just achieved.

Obviously, to get a winner's medal would've been superb and amazing. Same for a player such as Steven Gerrard, who'd been in such a place before. He'd played in a final. He'd already won a winner's medal, so he'd be absolutely devastated. For me it was different. Maybe winning before made playing easier for Steven, but I think he probably felt it harder because he knew what it felt like to win. But for me, it was my first time, and a year before that I had been in prison. I was devastated that we didn't win it, but I was ecstatic about what I had just achieved, and I had played ninety minutes in a Champions League final! I didn't come off, didn't get substituted. So it was both. It was a weird emotion. I was ecstatic and at the same time gutted.

I'd also given everything and I genuinely thought, 'Yeah, this is where everything is gonna change now. I'll probably play for England now. My life's going to be what every young boy dreams of.' I thought finally I could become a superstar! Become a player who knows where he can go next, because I was still young, in my mid-twenties, with the world at my feet.

But – and it just *would* happen to me – I got a little injury afterwards at Liverpool. I was out for three months and obviously wasn't in the team and didn't make the same progress under Rafa.

However, how many English players have played in a Champions League final? Not many have, and, for the past five years, our teams have been struggling to get through to the quarters, never mind the final.

It's a career high and, for me, myself, personally, I think it's a fantastic achievement. Meanwhile, I was basically trying to keep a lid on my emotions straight after the game and not show anyone this weird mix of feelings, which almost made me feel guilty.

Afterwards, the winning team do their bit on the pitch, get their medals. You watch them go up and you feel very empty. As we've seen, we got our medals, and just basically walked off. The manager will give his little team talk; we have a shower. You put it to the back of your mind, not up for celebrating, really, because you've just lost the Champions League final. We didn't lose in a bad way. It was two shitty goals and we just couldn't claim it back.

But then you get to the hotel and the wives and girlfriends are all there. They all get flown over the day before and they stay in a different hotel. So they were already over and had all watched the game together, so when we got back to the hotel they were all there waiting. And then they put on dinner and drinks: champagne, some beer. It looks like a little party in the hotel for the team and the team management, everyone involved in Liverpool: the players and their wives, young kids. But it's a weird feeling, because no one really feels in the mood. It's just to have a little drink, not a celebration. It's been a long season, we've done well to get to the Champions League final. It's just like a little farewell. Then you just go back to your rooms with your partners.

The next day, you prepare to leave the wives and girlfriends. They all go on a different coach from the players and team officials.

* * *

Not long after I went on holiday with some friends to Marbella and it had completely changed for me. The attention I got was incredible. There were a lot of Scousers there, anyway, but suddenly I felt like a big star, people all over me. It was as if Steven Gerrard were there rather than me. But, being me, I milked it and took full advantage of it! I'm sure my friends did, too, and they had become good wingmen!

I suddenly went from merely being a footballer playing for Liverpool, to being a big star and Man of the Match in a Champions League final. People look at you as being in a different grade because you played in that final. Suddenly, they're fawning all over you. You go VIP. The waiter's saying, 'Your table's waiting for you, Mr Pennant.'

My career was also taking off – or so I thought – because everyone was talking about an England call-up. The clubs, the papers, teammates, everyone. The closest I came was during the 2007/08 season. I got a slight hamstring injury and I was in the VIP area watching one of the games at Anfield. Steve McClaren was there. He was in charge of England then and had come up to me as I was walking down the stairs to go the area to sit down and watch the game. I caught him on the stairs and he said, 'What's wrong? Why aren't you playing?' I told him it was a hamstring injury. He then said, 'I know you're doing great. Keep going, you just need to keep going.'

And I was thinking, 'Fucking hell! About time! Jesus! Get in there! Come on!' Let me tell you, it was the best football match I've ever watched!

There was talk about it in the press. And I thought, 'Well, if you've got the press on your side, it's gonna happen, because the press can do anything! Come on!' But, sadly, it

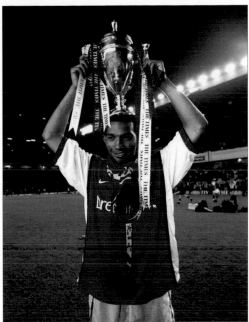

Above left: I kept this newspaper cutting about my transfer to Arsenal – been making headlines since day one!

© *The Daily Star*

Above right: Getting a taste of silverware: celebrating the FA Youth Cup final win over Coventry.

© *PA Images*

Below: A moment I'll never forget: scoring a hat-trick on my full Arsenal debut. . . with a world-class hangover!

© *REX*

Above: Arsenal vs United games at Old Trafford were always tasty. © *PA Images*

Below: Champagne celebrations after beating United in the Community Shield. I started on the right, surrounded an unreal 'Invincibles' era attack: Henry, Berkgamp, Fabregas, Reyes. What do you do against that? © *PA Images*

Above: Thierry Henry was by far the best player I ever played with, and one of the best I ever played against. Impossible to get the ball off him! Messi wasn't bad, though.

Below: Head to head with Ashley – no such thing as 'friends' on a football pitch!

Above and right:
Two good men – my
agent Sky, who is like
another father to me,
and Steve Bruce – a
true gent and the best
manager I worked
with. *© Getty and PA Images*

Left: My ankle tag
became almost as
famous as I was!

© PA Images

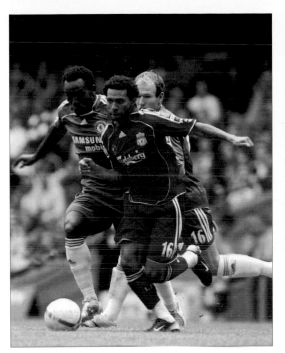

Above left: Playing against the best players is what makes this worthwhile.

© RFX

Above right: Focus… pure and simple.

© PA Images

Below: My dead-ball delivery was always a strong point, and usually never let me down in high-pressure situations.

© REX

The biggest occasion of all – the Champions League final. It doesn't get any tougher than playing against guys like Seedorf and Maldini. We were crushed to lose – even if I was proud of my own performance against a world-class side.

Left: As a pro footballer, beautiful women come with the territory – but none more beautiful than my wife, Alice Goodwin.

Below: Fast cars? Yeah, I've had a few. Maybe chroming the Aston was a bit much, though. . .

Above left: Two of my oldest and closest friends, Christopher and Anthony.

Above right: Some of the Pennant clan!

Below: Darkness and light: I've not always been an angel in my time, but I know I'm not a bad person either, despite what some newspapers would have you believe. There are two sides to every story.

just never did happen. Don't know whether the hierarchy were not sure about me and told McClaren not to pick me, but the call never came up.

I do feel as if the FA sometimes have a sway on managers over who gets to play – unless you are John Terry and you can do whatever you want and it doesn't matter. They seemed to turn a blind eye to everything and it was John Terry who called time on playing for England.

But, with me, all my off-the-field troubles took their toll and had a sway, for sure. That was at a time when the England team were fading a bit and a few big names were retiring. These days you have to play only three good games in the Premier League and you're in. It's crazy. So compare that to my being Man of the Match in the Champions League final. Well, it is mental.

I was thinking, 'What the fuck have I got to do to get recognised and even to be on the shortlist?' Going back, I can remember we played a game at Southampton and Sven-Göran Eriksson and his assistant were present. You would've thought it was a little Messi out there. I was literally getting the ball from our defence and going through and doing all sorts.

I can remember someone saying that Eriksson had told them, 'Jermaine Pennant was amazing that game. He's definitely one for the future. I'm going to keep an eye on him.' When you hear stuff like that it gives you a boost. But then the call never comes and you think, 'What more have I got to do?'

MENTAL

Someone can be good and get a call-up, but I've got to be absolutely amazing to get mentioned. And that's how it felt. And, when I was at Liverpool, it's as if I was to have the best season. No one apart from Pepe Reina played in that team more than I did that year.

Then the 2007/08 season started to go wrong for me. I got an injury and my career was halted with Liverpool, but I thought Rafa Benítez should've shown me a bit more respect. It was as if I'd missed a few games through injury and suddenly I was discarded.

It was then that I began to lose my head a little, because I was getting annoyed, pissed off, and I felt I wasn't being treated fairly. Subconsciously, I probably lost my way and didn't put so much effort in because I felt Rafa had it in for me.

I was fading away. Slowly, slowly, bit by bit. Not playing as much as I wanted to. Getting annoyed when seeing Dirk Kuyt playing on the right, thinking he couldn't do what I was doing.

It started to really get to me, and I was wondering what I needed to do. Why was Benítez now all of a sudden not wanting to play me? I was the same player I'd been four months ago, before the season finished.

Rafa would drive a player mad, not more so than actually during games. When you are playing and are on his side near the touchline, the amount of instruction he would shout was incredible. He would literally be telling you where to pass the ball. Where to run, where to go. Get back, go there, track back, do this, do that. It was like nothing that I've ever experienced under any other manager. I was thinking, 'Fucking hell, Rafa! I'm a professional footballer. You don't need to tell me where to pass the ball and who to.'

On the pitch, often I can see what's best. Ultimately you have to trust the players once they cross the white line. But with Rafa, it was constant directions. Just sometimes, he might as well have turned a player into an Xbox, dressed me up like RoboCop and put a picture of my face on it. I'm not a defensive midfielder. I'm not James Milner, who keeps it simple. I'm a flair player and do my own thing. But his constant instructions really restricted me. They stopped me from being free. He could never let me do my thing. When I was playing on the other side of the pitch, away from the dugout, I was thinking, 'Thank Christ for that – I can't hear him. Brilliant!' When you have so many instructions, it makes it so difficult. You've got some instructions and tactics in your mind and yet he's shouting even more at you. All of a sudden you're confused. You've got two sets of instructions in your mind and you're left wondering what to do. It means that, suddenly, you mess up with a simple pass because your mind is all over the place.

'I'm sure that even the likes of Pep Guardiola, who is very loud and animated on the touchline, wouldn't shout to Messi, Neymar and Suárez about where to pass and where to run. He wouldn't do that at Manchester City, either, with different players, whether they were world-class or not. Yes, he might be telling them about positions, telling them to tuck in or whatever. But not where to pass, where to run or where to go the whole time. Honestly, Rafa was a nightmare like that.

So, if you were on his side of the pitch, it was horrendous. It was such a relief when you swapped sides.

Out of all the managers I've played under, I would say he was the most difficult. It was always very tactical with him. He would try to get too clever with the game, even in training. It was a bit boring at times. He would do tactical moves without a football. He would stand on the halfway line, pretend he had a ball, then shout out numbers. 'One' would mean shuffling over to the left, 'two' would be push up, 'three' to the right-hand side, 'four' to drop back. Five, push up to the midfield. Then he would kick a ball and the whole team would drop back. I used to think, 'Fucking hell! This is shocking.' It could be so boring. He would take that into game situations as well, and would constantly shout instructions. Don't get me wrong, there's a time for instructions, but, when you're telling players where to pass the ball, then it's gone too far. If it's like that the whole time, why not just put yourself on the pitch and pass the ball where you want?

It was like playing as if you were a robot. He is definitely not a player's man. He is so regimented. You could come in sometimes and train and think, 'For fuck's sake, not again!' He was definitely close to the players. There were times when I would get so angry about how boring and repetitive training was that I would just lose it and shout, 'For fuck's sake – just give us a bit of a five-a-side!'

As a player, you just want a bit of fun, to make training good and lively. But, with Rafa, the training was so boring that you'd come in and all you'd want to do was slit your wrists! The amount of time in training that we'd do shape, tactics and nothing else! As a manger, you need to understand that it needs to be fun to keep the players interested and motivated. But doing the same things over and over makes you get bored and you probably don't listen in the end because of that. A little bit of spice here and there is good for the players. It's simple things such as five-a-sides that are, for a football player, like a dream. To get one with Rafa was like getting blood out of a stone.

We didn't have that many videos, but there were a lot of tactics for stopping their strengths, what we needed to do rather than saying, 'Right, this is our game plan. We know where we are good.' We had Steven Gerrard, Torres and Alonso; we had a good team and people feared us. It was so boring under Rafa. It was tactics, tactics, tactics and it would do your nut in after a while.

I think he thought he was too clever by half, too clever for the game. Some of the substitutions that he made were all about trying to prove how clever he was. But it was the players who were doing all the work. He probably thought it was *his* work – his training and tactics – that got the results. The reality was that the players were very, very good at that stage and I don't think he got the best out of them, and particularly that squad.

The only time I really had a conversation with him was the day I joined. I signed, then I joined up with the squad on pre-season and went to the training camp.

That was the only time I really spoke to him on a one-to-one basis. As I said before, he made me write down all my misdemeanours and all my faults. I wrote them all down and then just drew a big circle around girls! It was like a little brainstorm. He then said to me, 'What's the worst?' I just put down 'GIRLS' in capital letters and said all my problems started from there!

But, to be honest, I think one of my faults is that I let things eat away at me and get me down. And then I start thinking, 'Why am I here? Why am I trying hard, day in and day out, at training?' And I start cussing, and anyone can tell by looking at me that I've lost interest.

I'm not being professional and am probably sulking. But I've learned now. I know that, no matter what life or my football career throws at me, I've just got to suck it up and deal with it and keep going. If the manager doesn't play me in the last game, then all I want is an explanation, and Benítez was bad at that. There was no reasoning, such as that I needed a rest or that it was a long season, blah, blah. Just silence. That was so hard to take for someone who had been a star one minute, playing in the Champions League final, and then just discarded the next.

I do think I cope better now and down the years I've learned that these days I won't start sulking and throwing my dummy out the pram. I just now accept it. Be professional, I tell myself, and train hard as if I'm going to be playing. I learn from my mistakes. I know it may be late, but it should never be *too* late.

I was supposed to try to make a good career out here. I definitely learned from it, but at the time it really ate away at me and took over.

I never really had a full-on row with Rafa Benítez. The only managers I ever had full-on rows with were Steve Bruce and Tony Pulis. Rafa didn't really shout. He's never a man-to-man manager, so I never really had a row. It was just as well, probably! He never really pulled me into his office, but would just talk to me on a normal level. However, he never once said what I'd done wrong or if my training was not good enough. Not once.

I think Rafa lost his way a little at Liverpool and it was probably down to his losing one of his assistants, Pako Ayestarán. I think it was a big thing for the whole club, really, and not just Rafa, when he left in the summer of 2007. Everyone, all the players, loved Pako, so when he left it was a really bad spell for the club.

With Rafa, it is all about himself. It was either his way or no way. The man management was down to his staff. That was why, when Pako Ayestarán went, they had a parting of the ways and things started to go downhill a bit. I think you could trace the fault lines a little from where it went wrong.

MENTAL

It was a unique style of management and they worked so well together. They *were* together. It was so important for a partnership in terms of coaching and recovery, and, when they split up, it wasn't quite the same again.

It was in my last season when it all started to go wrong and I let myself go. After that season I hardly played at all. It was as if I were discarded, really. It felt as if I were training with the reserves sometimes, and things just got worse and worse. I started disliking Rafa, and obviously it came to that day when I had to renew my contract and I knew it was all over for me at Liverpool.

They loaned me out to Portsmouth and I knew there was no future at Liverpool because, even though my contract was up, they were going to let me run it down while out on loan. Clubs don't really do that. That's what they thought of me.

I wasn't needed. I wasn't playing. And yet the funny thing is, there were talks before the Portsmouth move of my going to Real Madrid. Juande Ramos, the manager who had been in charge of Tottenham, was in charge at Real Madrid and suddenly the biggest club in the world wanted to sign me. It was incredible.

Sky Andrew called me up and said, 'Jermaine, listen. I can't believe it.' 'What?' I'm saying to him. 'Tell me!' He said, 'Real Madrid.' 'What do you mean about Real Madrid?' 'They wanna take you.' 'Brilliant. Yeah, let's do it!'

RICK PARRY: We got a call from Real Madrid and, bearing in mind his contract was running down, it was a very attractive deal. For every player, it's a dream move when Real Madrid come in. It would have been the chance to become the next Laurie Cunningham. But it did fizzle out quite quickly. I think there was an issue with Jermaine being Cup-tied for the Champions League but the interest was there and genuine.

SKY ANDREW: It was unbelievable. He's at Liverpool, in the last six months of his contract and can leave for free at the end. Rick Parry called me and he said, 'Are you sitting down? We've agreed a fee with Real Madrid.' I couldn't believe it. Rick Parry told me they'd organised a plane to pick us up to take Jermaine for a medical in Madrid. Jermaine wasn't playing at Liverpool. I rang him up and said, 'You're going to Real Madrid.' He asked me, 'Do they want me to play?' I had to say no. The manager at Real Madrid was Juande Ramos, who had been manager at Sevilla and Tottenham. Ramos was just looking for someone to be on the bench, to come in as cover. I told him that he wouldn't play. He said, 'How much are they going to pay me, then?' They were offering a three-year deal. It went on for a while and in the end they took Julien Faubert from West Ham. He went to Real Madrid and played about ten minutes for the rest of the season. That would have been Jermaine and, when Jermaine's not playing, all hell breaks loose. But, to be honest, you just don't know how things work out. He had the chance to go to Real Madrid and didn't go.

It was all good, all kind of agreed, but it wasn't agreed with the manager, Juande Ramos.

Whoever was doing the deal was doing it behind the manager's back. The sporting director or whoever had set up a deal without consulting the manager, so, when it got to the manager, he pulled the plug on it. I was devastated! And it came out in the press, as well, that I was joining Real Madrid. And Sky said they did a deal, but they didn't consult the manager and Ramos started kicking up a fuss, and so it didn't happen. I felt so disappointed. It had been built up – and then it was all off.

The next thing that came up was Portsmouth. So I'd gone from joining Real Madrid to Portsmouth! It didn't feel like the best career move at the time.

It was still the Premier League, though, and I was thinking, 'Just get me playing till the end of the season when my Liverpool contract runs out and then I can go.'

* * *

So I went to Portsmouth and Tony Adams was in charge. He was great, but he could get angry. I don't remember who we were playing but we were playing shit, and someone chirped up when he was giving us all a rollicking. He booted the bin and bent it in half! He could explode!

It was weird, because I kept on running into Peter Crouch. Crouchie had been at Liverpool and here he was at Portsmouth. We linked up really well, he the big striker and I the small winger. Glen Johnson was there and we had a team full of good players and loads of good banter. If you've got that in your team, then generally you'll do well because the players are happy. Every day there were wisecracks; it was so funny.

One thing we used to do on a Friday was ensure that the worst player in five-a-side had to drive a three-wheeler – like the car from the sitcom *Only Fools and Horses*. Basically, you had to drive one of those to the stadium on a match day, driving through all the fans, and all you would hear was, 'Look at him in that car!' Everyone was cracking up. They couldn't believe it. It was just ridiculous. But it was great fun.

The facilities weren't great, though. It wasn't Premier League standards for sure but, to be fair, the lads just got on with it and made the best of it. The stadium was bad, the training ground even worse. Completely outdated. We had no idea that the club was going to pot and was on the brink of financial meltdown. All that was a bit later. We were having too much of a good time to notice the signs, to be honest.

MENTAL

I can remember one great thing we used to do. We called it the Tuesday Club. In England, at a lot of clubs, you get Wednesdays off. So, one Tuesday, the lads arranged to meet up at the local. We agreed to have a few beers, then go to someone's house and play poker. Then someone else says we've all got to go in fancy dress. So, in the middle of the afternoon on a random Tuesday, we turn up in this little local boozer all done up in fancy dress.

We all had to choose and say what we were going as; someone went as a lobster and I was the biggest Gingerbread Man you've ever seen!

CHAPTER 8

PARKING THE CAR

I had thirteen months in Spain, some good times, bad times and wild times.

But all some people ever want to know when they talk about my time at Real Zaragoza is the story of my leaving a Porsche behind when I left Spain to go back to England. In fact, that's all they ever talk about. It was big headline news – yes, really – and if you Google it now you'll find some headlines along the lines of, 'Footballer forgets he owns a Porsche'. Well, despite my many crazy antics down the years, that isn't what happened.

I can laugh myself now, because I've heard so many different versions: that I left the car running, that I forgot I owned it, that I just abandoned it. I've done some pretty stupid things – but I'm not *that* bloody stupid!

So, let's put the record straight once and for all. And I promise you that this is the real version of a story that has been changed, exaggerated and completely made up so many times.

The car was a Porsche Cayenne, one of those jeeps. And, believe me, it was too expensive even for *me* to forget about! I'd had a year in Spain. It was coming to an end and I was hoping to get back to England. So I was waiting around for a few days, hoping something would happen, that I'd get a move back. But, with many last-minute deals, they really are done by the skin of your teeth.

I got the call on transfer-deadline day, 31 August 2010, telling me I had to fly to Manchester to go to Stoke for a medical and to join them on loan.

There was hardly any time, so I had to jump in the car, my Porsche Cayenne, drive to Zaragoza station, jump on the train to Madrid and catch a flight from there to Manchester. I pulled into the station, jumped on the train to Madrid, flew to Manchester. But when I say pulled into the station, I mean pulled into the station with the train on the platform and I thought, 'Oh, shit – I'm going to miss it.'

I had to jump out of the car, run for my life for the train and get on. I just made it! But I knew by then that the chances of my going back to Zaragoza – even though Stoke was only a loan deal – were very slim. I thought I'd leave it there for a while, look for an apartment, come back and get my stuff at some point.

So, I deliberately left the key inside the glove compartment together with the car-park ticket. If I needed to come back, then sweet, no problem, I'd sort it out. If I didn't, I could phone my friend Fernando, a translator, who was supposed to teach me Spanish, who became my mate during my time at Real Zaragoza.

A few weeks later, I messaged him and said, 'Look, mate, when you can, get my car, it's been there for about five weeks now, maybe six, so when you get my car, move it, put it in my garage or your garage, pay for my ticket and I'll transfer you the money.'

'Sure. No problem,' he says. 'Yeah, where is it? How am I going to get it? Where's the key?'

I told him, 'Don't worry, the car's open. It's inside.'

And he went crazy! 'What? Are you fucking crazy! It's a Porsche Cayenne!'

I went, 'Yeah, it's Zaragoza, though, it's safe.'

I've also seen another version of the story that it was a hire car and I was still paying for it, even though I'd gone back. That's wrong as well. I'd bought the car, bought it outright, so I owned it.

The biggest thing was, I think, that the security people at the station got a bit suspicious because the car had been there for six weeks. It had not moved. They may have thought it was possibly some sort of terrorist act. They started to look into it and obviously do background checks – and it came back to me.

My address was linked to the club, so they've contacted the club and then, obviously, it got all mixed up. Somehow, through whatever channel or means, it got out to the press in Spain and then the British press picked up the story.

Next thing you know, the story was that I left my car for six months and then the club called me to remind me that I had *got* a car. Come on! Supposedly, I then said, 'Oh, shit! Yeah, my Porsche. I totally forgot I owned it.' So the story became that I had left my car and had no idea that I owned it. I've even heard another one: that I left the engine running in the car park, and it kept going until it ran out of petrol. That's a good one, but, again, I'm not that fucking stupid.

From what I remember – and I *do* remember – I pulled up, there was the train, I jumped out of the car and ran for said train.

But, looking back, I realise that I could have had no idea of how much fuss all this was going to cause. When I left the car, I didn't know if I'd be coming back. But I never forgot it. I didn't leave it running. I didn't forget to pay for the car or the parking. However, some people remember me only as the footballer who forgot he owned a Porsche. Sadly for them, it was not like that at all.

SKY ANDREW: He always had something to do. He was always rushing around, a flight to catch, train to get or whatever. He was desperately rushing to leave Zaragoza to sign for Stoke. He got out of the car, could see the train pulling into the station. He was in such a rush – and he'd never admit this – but he got out of the car, left the engine running and it took two weeks for the petrol to run out! He denies it. But that's what happened.

That just about summed up my time in Spain. It was a strange time. I enjoyed it. It was a new challenge for me, going abroad, which is not something a lot of English players do in their careers.

But, after what happened at Liverpool and then Portsmouth, it was something I really looked forward to and was totally different.

***

Yes, I was looking forward to it, because I like the way Spanish football is played and I thought it would suit me really well. I mean, it's technical, it's not physical. You get a little bit more time on the ball.

That summer, the summer of 2009, I was available on a free transfer because my contract had expired at Liverpool. Someone obviously got in touch with my agent Sky Andrew and, because I was a free transfer, they said Real Zaragoza were interested. They had just got promoted and obviously wanted a good marquee signing, a statement kind of player, a signing from a big club, but they did not want to have to pay a lot of money to boost their squad.

Sky and I flew over there for negotiations. We were back and forth, with meeting after meeting, offer after offer, and then they came with their last offer, and we said no, it wasn't enough.

So we walked off, straight out of the office, walking away from the biggest deal of my life. We got to the lift and looked at each other and said, 'Shit!' We were both cursing, thinking, 'We should've said yes!' And then the lift went ping. We were about to get in, about to leave, go home, and I was thinking, 'What have I turned down here?' We didn't want to go, but we didn't want to look weak, either. Then the general manager came running out. 'Whoa, Sky! Sky, stop! Come back! We talk, we talk!'

SKY ANDREW: I had inserted a clause that if he didn't play a certain number of games then he could go on a free. I always tell players that it's always about the clauses. Again, we had a problem because he left Liverpool and most Premier League clubs saw him as a risk. He was earning big money, wanted big money, and a colleague of mine put me onto Real Zaragoza. We had a couple of meetings, then flew to Spain for a meeting.

I'm not sure the average fan knows this, but in Spain they pay the salary in two blocks, once every six months. In England, it's different and you get paid monthly, and I told Zaragoza they had to pay him monthly. He wasn't good with money. No matter how much he was being paid, he was always playing catch-up. In Spain, they give you a small amount to live on and then pay you every six months. Jermaine didn't want to do it that way, and he's sitting there arguing with the director of football, who was adamant they didn't want to do monthly wages. We came out, I told him we were going to say we were walking away. This was while knowing we had nothing in England. It was this or nothing.

We got into the lift, he was sweating and was panicking when he said: 'What are we going to do now?' He was panicking and shouting, 'What are we going to do now!' He'd played it all cool, got in the lift, standing there as if he had five clubs lined up, and he was going crazy.

The lift went down, doors opened and there was someone at the bottom waiting for us, took us back upstairs, and we signed a two-year contract. Did the deal.

We ended up getting what we wanted and that worked out to be the biggest deal in my career. That all went well. Signed everything. Pre-season went well. Everything was good.

***

The manager at Zaragoza was Marcelino García Toral. He was really good, I liked him. Everything was going smoothly. I was looking good. I struggled a little bit at first with the language, because I didn't know a word of Spanish. They got someone in for the start who could speak English, show me around, do little bits of communicating when needed. It was a young guy called Fernando, who I mentioned earlier. In meetings he was my translator. But football really is a worldwide language. You basically can just show, and the manager points and gets his message across. The difficult stuff then would be translated for me. In the meantime, I was learning the basics: 'left', 'right', 'up', 'down', 'come across', 'tuck in', 'pass', 'run', 'man on'. All that sort of stuff.

Then my instructor and I ended up just being friends. There was a bit of tutoring, and then going out, partying and just enjoying life! He became my good buddy there.

There was another player, Franck Songo'o, who played at Portsmouth, joined Zaragoza, could speak English as well, and quickly we became big mates – in fact, he became my closest friend there. So, in actual training he was telling me what was going on, what was the drill and what was not. We lived in the same apartment blocks. We got on well, very well. He was a bit of lad, too, at the time, a bit like me, which I don't think was a good thing!

The lifestyle in Spain probably depends where you are. If you're in Barcelona, Madrid, Seville, Valencia, the good cities, I can imagine it would be hectic, top notch; but where I was, Zaragoza, is in the middle of Spain, it's old and it's cultured. It's proper Spanish. You won't see foreigners and multicultural people. It's just traditional Spanish people.

It was different with the siesta in the afternoon. At certain times I'd be starving mid-afternoon, saying: 'Ah, I want to go grab a bite to eat and I go to the shops.' Then all I'd see was a sign saying, 'Closed, siesta, we open at five.' I was thinking, 'For fuck's sake – just feed me! Wake up!'

I had to start getting used to that. Closed at twelve, open at five. It was crazy. It was a bit annoying after training, when you're starving and everything is closed. You couldn't even get a bun!

It was quiet in Zaragoza, whereas, if you go to Barcelona or Madrid, then it's obviously all going off. But, yes, it was a good way of life, for sure. I did enjoy it, but the language barrier was difficult. I'm sure Gareth Bale is having a whale of a time in Madrid. I think he can speak a bit of Spanish, which always helps. Meanwhile, I learned a little. '*Dos cerveza, por favor.*' Two beers…That would get me as far as I needed to go! If I went out with people they'd say I didn't speak Spanish and I guess quickly people make a big thing of that, and start saying you're not settling in and so on.

But the football was good. We started off well. Obviously, we were a new team and we got a good result, 1–0 against Tenerife, which went out live on Sky Sports. I played well in that game. But after that, it was obviously difficult for a team just promoted, and we struggled badly.

It was a fight for relegation and then the manager got

sacked – the one who had brought me in. Then the youth team manager, José Aurelio Gay, was brought in. He didn't fancy a few players, and made changes. I got a few injuries and then I started to find life getting very difficult.

The thing about me is that, when I'm not playing, when I know – or at least think – I *should* be, that's when I struggle. When I'm not in my comfort zone.

So there I was, in Spain, not in the team, fed up, and I'd got no real family or old friends there. I just couldn't nip out and see the boys.

When you're playing, it keeps your mind off things because you've got a job to do. But when you're not you find yourself saying, 'For fuck's sake! Why am I not playing?' It was then that I started to get frustrated because I was twenty-seven, was still learning, still trying to improve. I was genuinely training hard, working hard.

At the same time, my pal Franck was not playing, either, and we were both getting really annoyed and fed up. So we just started to go out all the time, taking a trip to Barcelona or getting a train to Madrid.

We had some good times while we were there, believe me. Not just Franck and I, but also some of the younger lads. But the nightlife in Zaragoza is really bad, truly awful. I remember going out in Zaragoza one night and it was like a student night out – proper 'studenty'. It really wasn't good.

But we'd go out, some of the younger lads and I, and next thing you know we could be having a drink in a bar or whatever and there would be girls all around us. I couldn't have a conversation because I couldn't speak Spanish very well, if at all, early on.

Honestly, they could be calling me all the names under the sun, saying I'm a right tosspot, and I'd be just going, '*Si, si, si.*' Agreeing with everything and nodding my head.

There was one night when we had a few drinks and took some girls back to my apartment. The girls couldn't speak English, I couldn't speak Spanish, but I didn't need to say anything. I could just grab a girl, take her into my bedroom, close the door, draw the curtains and that was it. No conversation. Just sex.

I figured that, basically, I could just grab a girl, say that we were going to have sex, *now* (maybe they could understand *that*!), and they'd be up for it. It was pretty clear that we *were* going to do it – and that was that. Some of the younger lads kept opening the door while we were at it. I kept saying, 'Nah, stop that!' It was just crazy.

And, believe me, one time I got caught out in a way you would not believe! It happened really badly only once. I'm sure the lads had suspicions. I had been on holiday to Las Vegas the previous summer and we'd met some girls from Canada. We had a great time and even after we went home I stayed in touch, kept chatting away, and told them that, if they ever came to Spain, my pal Frankie and I would show them a good time.

One day they said they were coming over to Barcelona, so I promised to meet up with them, take them to spots, and then I told Franck, 'Look, man, there's four decent girls coming over from Canada. I'm all over this. Are you up for it?' Needless to say, Franck agreed.

The trouble was that, when we arranged to meet them, we were planning a big night out in Barcelona – and yet we had training the next day. I was thinking, 'What can we do?'

So we thought we'd go to Barcelona – which is about a hundred and sixty miles from Zaragoza – and just get a hotel. Then we'd get the first train home at about 6.30 in the morning. We'd get back easily by 9.30 a.m., at the latest 10 a.m., and then training's not until . . . Well, you get the picture. Easy.

But that was without banking on the night out being absolutely hectic! It was wild, absolutely crazy. So, after training, we got the train to Barcelona, did a bit of shopping and then we got ready for the night out. We went to the nightclub owned by Patrick Kluivert. It was crazy. As a footballer, you get into the VIP area, no problem. Then there were girls I didn't know, guys I'd never met, all shouting, '*Eh, amigo!*' I was loving it, playing up to it, and next thing you know everyone is '*amigo*', getting on, and the night is just wild.

So we were in the club until very late and had a bit of sushi or whatever to eat, but otherwise it was just drinking, drinking, drinking. We got a cab back to the hotel at about four or five in the morning, I went to my room with one of the Canadian girls I'd met in Vegas; Franck took another girl back to his room.

Luckily, I had set the alarm for 6 a.m. I woke up but was thinking, 'Oh, God, I can't do this!' But Franck kept banging on my door. I jumped in the shower, got some clothes on, said goodbye (the girl was still asleep) and off we went.

We somehow got the train, but I felt like death, absolute death. And there was no way I could go to training without getting into shit because I couldn't open my eyes and I stank like a brewery. The amount of alcohol I'd drunk was an absolute disgrace, so I thought the best thing to do was to ring the doc and say I'd got the shits. So I sent a text at 9 a.m., an hour before training, saying I'd got the runs, felt really bad, really sick. I thought sending it early would do the trick, as it wouldn't look so suspicious.

Frankie knew *he* couldn't phone in and say he was off as well, or it would look dodgy. They'd know something was going on. 'Oh, fuck it!' he said. 'I've got to go in!'

I said, 'You go in, and I'll stay home saying I've got the shits, that I'm puking up. So I'd sent the text, but the problem was that I was still on the train when I sent it. Next thing I know, they've said they're going to send a doctor out to see me.

I was thinking, 'Oh, for fuck's sake!' Jesus! How do I get myself in these situations?

Next thing, I've got a doctor ringing asking for my address. I'm screaming at the train to go faster. The doc keeps ringing and ringing. But I just ignore it. I get home and there's a message from the translator saying the doctor has been round and no one was in.

I just said, 'Ah, do you know what? I was so sleepy I didn't even hear the doorbell ring.' By this time I'd got home and so said, 'Send him back round.' He replied, 'Ah, no don't worry about it, don't worry about it.' I think they knew, knowing what I'm like!

The next day I went in and they said, 'Do you feel all right?' The club doctor checked my stomach. I said I felt a little better. I thought I should be all right for training I'd be fine, would just take loads of tablets.

They couldn't actually prove anything, so there was not a lot they could do. I made up the excuse that I just didn't hear the doorbell. So sorry, I said, that I didn't hear you ringing. I was fast asleep.

So that was *that* particular incident. There were a few others like it. There was one that saw me getting fined. Basically, I was injured and they said everyone was off duty for two or three days. I think it was international break or something. So I was in all week, having treatment, didn't have one day off. That's how it generally works in football: if you're injured, there are no days off. You just come in for treatment.

So, when the break came round, I was hoping for a bit of time off. I'd made some plans and I was thinking, 'Ah, two days off. Fantastic!' Next thing, I'm being told that I'm due in tomorrow for treatment. And said, 'What? I can't!' And I properly kicked off. 'This is shit. I've been in all week, not had a day off. The others had a day off and now they've got another two days off. This is bullshit.' Blah, blah, blah. I got kind of angry. And then I spoke to the general manager and said, 'Look! I need two days off. I need to go home to England to sort some house stuff out. I've got some bits and bobs to do. It's important.' And he said, 'Ah, OK, OK, you can have two days off, just make sure you're back in time.' I said: 'Yeah, perfect.'

I needed the two days off because there were the closing parties in Marbella. 'Wicked!' I thought. 'I've got Marbella with the boys. I've made it – *yeah!*'

Having told management I needed to go to England, I'd actually stayed in Spain. I thought I'd be fine. It was in Marbella. I didn't think it would be connected and I never thought they'd find out.

So I was there for two days, sitting on a sunbed, as you do in Marbella. You don't need the details because anyone who goes to Marbella knows it's about girls and champagne parties from when your eyes open in the morning to when you fall asleep at night. Then came the last night. I obviously had a very heavy one, and had to get up in the morning.

All my mates were flying back to England and I was flying back to Zaragoza. So everyone thought it was funny to leave me fast asleep on the sofa. Really funny. There was no chance of my getting up; I didn't even know where I was when I woke up. So they left me fast asleep and I missed the flight back and missed training.

I was in such a bad state that I didn't even message anybody to say where I was. They just didn't have a clue where I was or hear from me. I was supposed to be in on the Monday, so I landed back later that day, having missed training. Then I slept the rest of Monday and woke up Tuesday *night*! So I'd missed training all Tuesday, as well. And, to be honest, I couldn't have gone in on the Tuesday because I couldn't have faced all the shit I would get. Add to this the fact that I couldn't physically go in because I couldn't move owing to the state I was in.

Sky was calling me all the time. 'What the fuck are you playing at? They know you were in Marbella. They've got photos of you getting it on with some babe. You told them you was going to England to sort out some important shit and you're in your shorts with your tattoos out, getting it on with girls on your arm.'

I was still trying to deny it all, but the nightclub photographer had taken the pictures of me there. I'd been properly rumbled!

Sky was shouting, 'You're on the website. Do you think they're stupid? You're on the website; you're in Spain; you're Jermaine Pennant; you've just signed for Zaragoza. It's big news! People are going to know and going to talk. It's going to get about. What's wrong with you?'

There I was, thinking I'd kept my head down and not been seen by anyone. But I've been caught out really badly.

To be honest, I made Sky's life a complete nightmare – a hundred per cent. I actually don't now how he's still standing. I've definitely taken at least ten years off his life! I don't know quite how, but we're still buddies through thick and thin. He's been fantastic for me even when I've probably not been very good for myself. But he's always been like a father figure for me, really helped me.

**

That was a really bad time for me in Spain. It kind of just faded away for me at Real Zaragoza. And all the time I was being paid an absolute fortune. To be honest, I didn't behave well. I didn't take it seriously enough, because I was too busy having the time of my life. But that couldn't last for ever.

After the Marbella incident, I finally went in on the Wednesday and had a meeting, I apologised, but they fined me a month's wage! That's big money. In England, the maximum you get fined is two weeks' worth; in Spain, they fined me a month's, so it was €136,000.

That was a very expensive trip to Marbella!

The problem was that there was no way back into the team, no way back for me at the club, and it just kind of faded away.

The new manager had come in and my attitude back then wasn't what it is now. It wasn't good for me in that situation. Not being in my comfort zone, being in another country, not playing – you can imagine what was going to happen. So, to be honest, it kind of did! But with me, it tends to end up being even worse. And they were paying me absolute fortunes while, as a club, they were strapped for cash.

It's strange in Spain because, unlike in England, where you get paid every month, they pay you every six months. All players get is living money every month – maybe

€10,000 – and then, at six months, they get the balance of their salary. I have no idea why clubs do it. But I made sure I got paid every month and insisted on that as a condition of signing. It's what I was used to and would have found it difficult living only on monthly living expenses, with the lifestyle I had. In Spain, however, it's what everyone was used to. But, obviously, the other players found out how I was being paid, that I was being paid each month, maybe getting some special treatment, and resented it. They didn't like it. Then, on top of that, they were hearing that I was caught in Marbella, had seen some pictures of me spraying champagne all about, birds on my right and left arms and thinking I was too flash and living it up.

It's strange because, in that situation, they didn't ignore me, but maybe there's some resentment. They don't say it to your face, but subconsciously they hold it against you for being on more money and whatever. It's probably the same at every club with a player or two.

I was one of the best players at the club, a good player for the team and, as I keep saying, I get along with everyone. No one dislikes me as such. I didn't give it big time, or come into training thinking that I was better than everyone else. I just took the piss a bit too much, really. There was a just a point where I thought, 'You know what? This isn't working.' The team were struggling and I was getting frustrated; my motivation was getting lower and lower with each week that went by.

I think my worst moment on a football pitch was when

we were beaten 6–1 by Barcelona in the Nou Camp when I was at Real Zaragoza. I just couldn't touch the ball. It was all going wrong for me and the club. That was right up there with getting sent off while I was at Liverpool and we played Porto away. Two yellow cards. I was in the changing rooms, knowing that the game was still going on and I was praying that we would not lose. Putting all the players in danger in such a big, high-stakes game was probably one of the worst moments. I've been sent off only once or twice in a major competition, and that was one of them.

I was sitting in there just praying, scared to go out and look at the score. I was thinking to myself, 'Please don't lose this game, please don't lose this game.'

Then all of the players came in and I apologised to them all. We came out with a 1–1 draw and we got to the Champions League final. That was probably the worst moment. They were both stupid cards. I went for the ball, it was going out of play, the player fell over and the ref gave me another yellow – and that was it.

I don't take disappointments and setbacks well, and, by the following August, I knew it was time for me to go, and then we agreed that I could leave Real Zaragoza on loan. By that stage, I wasn't fussy. I was just keen to get home, keen to get back to England and start playing again. It hadn't gone well on the pitch for Real Zaragoza. It was a difficult season for the club and I suppose that I didn't help.

I was speaking to my agent Sky all the time, trying to push him into getting me out of there. Sorry but, after just

the Saturday. He'd come back into the dressing room, apparently fuming after a really shit performance, and said, 'Right, I'll see you Sunday.'

So the boys were protesting with, 'What? It's our night out.' James Beattie was the loudest and shouted: 'Oh, for fuck's sake!'

Pulis had been in the shower, heard that, supposedly dropped his towel and, stark bollock-naked, went up to Beattie to try to headbutt him!

So you've got a naked Premier League football manager trying to headbutt his striker!

Pulis missed. Beattie went to swing for him and didn't really connect. Then everyone piled in to try to break it up.

Pulis was then swearing his head off, effing and blinding, and, from that point on, Beattie became history. Even though it was before my time it used to get told to every new player as a cautionary tale, and it probably made them a bit bloody scared of Tony Pulis.

Our relationship was a bit feisty at times and, all the time, I was thinking, 'I'd better watch myself or he'll try to nut me!'

He is well known for his long-ball style, direct football, hitting the big guy and, after a while, it got so boring playing and training like that. I remember one training session when we were doing shape on a Friday, working out our pattern for the game the next day. Then he told someone to hit the ball long, and I just snapped. It was one long ball too many for me. 'For fuck's sake!' I shouted.

Then Tony stopped training, turned round to one of the coaches and screamed, 'What did he say? What did he fucking say?'

Then he walked over to me and there I was, thinking, 'Are you going to fire me? Are you going to have a swing or try to headbutt me like I heard you tried with James Beattie? Should I be on my toes like Floyd Mayweather?' He was livid but I was cracking up inside thinking about that story.

If Tony Pulis was to try to sign me now, it could be for the best contract in the world and I still wouldn't go. I'm happy to let bygones be bygones. We've moved on. He's a nice family-oriented man, even if he had one hell of a temper.

But his training was horrendous! It was so, so boring. It would drive me nuts!

My relationship with Pulis was like a rollercoaster. He was all high and mighty at first, very strict and no-nonsense, but I didn't mind him. All the players warned me to give it three months, then I'd find out for myself and see how bad he was. After time it wore on and on and it started to get so boring. The same old training, day after day – it was awful. It was just tactics, tactics, shape, shape! You would wake up and walk into training thinking, 'Oh, for fuck's sake – we've got this shit again.' You'd then lose all your motivation because you knew what you were going into.

And none of them enjoyed it. None of them. We just

got on with it. It was the same for Ryan Shawcross, Glenn Whelan, everybody. They all hated it. They're all seen as disciples of Tony Pulis, his players, yet they all hated it.

The big saving grace was that they were such a good bunch of lads and we dug deep and performed well on the pitch. We worked hard and that's why we were such a hard team to beat, especially at Stoke's Britannia Stadium.

The banter in the dressing room was great at Stoke, some of the best I've been involved in. But as soon as the clock reached half-past ten, everyone was thinking, 'Oh, shit, here we go again!' You were counting down the time until it was finished and you were back in the shower.

We just wanted something else, something to break the boredom. All he was doing was shape, shape, shape. Hit the ball long into the channel. Day after day. I was desperate for some shooting practice, crossing, anything to break the monotony.

To be honest, going to Stoke was a bit of a culture shock. I was used to the Premier League and the English style of football. It's tough and physical. But being at Stoke was different again. It was tough, demanding and very different from what I'd come from in Spain. I went from having time on the ball, being able to express myself and not really having to defend too much, to then being a groundhog under Tony Pulis. It was like being treated like a dog.

At first, it was good to be back in England, playing in the

Premier League, and I was enjoying it. But the rest of the lads all kept saying, 'Just give it three months.'

Sure enough, the training got worse and worse. More repetitive. The style of football, too, was awful, not enjoyable. I had a stiff neck from looking up at the sky. I was thinking, 'Here comes the next rocket launcher!' You're waiting for the ball to come down from outer space and look up again. 'My neck's gone again! Oh, wait, here we go, it's coming in my direction.'

During the first season, I signed on loan and I hit it off with the fans. They took to me instantly and they got right behind me at the Britannia, so it was a great feeling. It went so well in those first few months that Stoke wanted to sign me permanently in January, because I was playing every game on one wing with Matty Etherington on the other wing.

We made it a nightmare for a lot of teams, bombing down the wings and getting the ball in the box for Peter Crouch or Kenwyne Jones. And, to be honest, that's all Tony Pulis told us to do. Get the ball out wide, hit the channels and then launch it into the box for the big guys. It wasn't pretty at all, but the assists that I got for Kenwyne and Crouchie were amazing.

The funny thing was – and the fans of both clubs will tell you – there was such a rivalry between Stoke and one of my former clubs, Arsenal. It got really bad after Ryan Shawcross broke Aaron Ramsey's leg with a horrific challenge. But, to be honest, I think there was some tension before that because of Pulis and Arsène Wenger. They played totally different football and, clearly, there was no love lost between them. But, even though I'd played for Arsenal and liked the club as well as a lot of the people there, the fans always gave me so much stick. And, if they do that to me, then I will often rise to the bait and try to show them. I didn't mind it one bit if it made me play better.

The Arsenal fans were relentless when they came to the Britannia, singing songs with words such as 'You should be in jail!' followed by 'Ashley's boyfriend'. I remember scoring against Arsenal. We won 3–1, we were playing towards the away end and the feeling was amazing. They all went quiet and it was if I could see a single fan staring back at me when I looked into the crowd. They didn't like me.

So, instead of just running back towards the halfway line or dugout, I ran past the goal, round the goal, along the touchline to where the fans were. And I was shouting back at them, 'I can't hear you singing now!' Then I ran over to *our* fans, just to milk it some more.

They didn't like it at all, but we kept beating them. We had a real hold over them at the Britannia. I can remember having some argy-bargy with Jack Wilshere. I gave him some back and then got substituted to stop me from getting a second yellow card, as I'd already been booked and I didn't want to miss any games, as we were on a Cup run. But I really enjoyed those ding-dong battles against Arsenal because it felt as if had something to prove.

GARY PENNANT: I'm so proud of him. He's had a difficult life, a colourful life. But he has made me so proud. Going back to his early life, I didn't have much, but I made sure that he had everything – the best boots, the best gym trainers. Everything to do with football, he had the best.

The highlight of his career was for Notts County. He came on, was the youngest player to play for County and the right-back got sent off because Jermaine just tormented him and he hacked him down and got sent off. That one and him signing for Liverpool. I could have died then, happy.

We speak not as often as I would like, but that's more of a Pennant thing. The males in our family find it hard to phone. It's a man thing rather than a problem between him and me. We're close, from that bond from having him since he was three. I'm so proud of him and I tell him that quite often – how proud I am.

The FA Cup run in 2011 was definitely the best part of my time at Stoke, without a shadow of a doubt. The 2007 Champions League final had been a great moment in my career, but the FA Cup semifinal, when we beat Bolton 5–0, is right up there in my career highlights. It was a massive high. For us at Stoke, that was a terrific game: getting into the final itself, the buzz around Stoke, the way we were preparing for it, the way we won, the fans' reaction and getting into the final for the first time ever – all of this amounted to a brilliant moment in my career.

I played well. We did well as a team. I set up Kenwyne Jones from dribbling the ball from the halfway line and it was the day when everything came together. We couldn't do anything wrong. They didn't turn up. The occasion got to them, but it definitely didn't get to us.

We actually had a good team at Stoke, which made it a bit frustrating that we didn't always seem to *try* to play football. When we were on song, we could beat anyone. We also had some good individuals as well. That set us up really; that made us get into the final, which got us into the Europa League the following season. That was a great achievement as well. We made history when I was at Stoke.

It felt as if we were onto a good thing after we beat West Ham in the quarterfinal. It was a tough game. We won 2–1. Then the semifinal at Wembley was one of my best experiences in football.

We played Bolton and we won 5–0 in the semifinal. Bolton didn't turn up. I think the occasion got to them and we were up for it. The build-up around Stoke and among the fans was huge, even for the semifinal, because, as a club, that's the furthest we'd been in the FA Cup for a long, long time.

Then, the build-up to the final was even bigger. It felt really humungous! Tony Pulis did something really strange – but it worked. He organised a day trip to London. We went, and did a walk around the stadium a week or so before the final, so we could get used to the surroundings. It was what you might call a bit of a stadium tour. We looked around the place, had a walk on the pitch, got a feel for Wembley. It really helped us get our focus. It sounded like a wind-up at first, but it turned out to be a great idea.

I think it helped with the nerves because, we knew we were in for a really tough game as Manchester City had become a force to be reckoned with. They were huge favourites, and in a way that helped, too, because we had nothing to lose. They were expected to win, and we were expected to get battered – everyone was saying by three or four. That helped take a little bit of pressure off and I think put a bit more pressure on Manchester City.

I can't remember exactly where we stayed; I think it was near King's Cross. But it was such a nerve-racking experience. You have your last meal before bed. I can't remember who I shared with but I remember struggling to sleep because of nerves, and then I woke up, was stretching, trying to get loose for the game, and I looked a right idiot lying there, stretching my legs out.

We went into the final with our game plan and we did well. We had some chances. I had a chance; Kenwyne Jones had a chance; and we ended up losing 1–0. But we all stood up to be counted and, for me, it was an emotional day as well. I think I shed a few tears when the final whistle went.

It felt as if we had been on a long journey, done really well to get there, but just couldn't turn the tide and put the opposition under enough pressure for us to win the game and cause an upset.

It was strange, because I cried after the FA Cup final but didn't do so after the Champions League game. Maybe it's because of the tradition or being at Wembley, but it felt different being at the home of English football.

People talk about the FA Cup final being special and the world's greatest cup competition, and – as a player, even as a modern-day player – I can promise you that it really is special. Wembley, the day out, the FA Cup. It's special.

I also think it helped put Stoke on the map that season. It was the first time the club had ever reached an FA Cup final. We made history that day and all of that made it a big, emotional occasion.

Of course, the Champions League final was bigger globally, but Liverpool had already won it five times and so it felt as if this Cup final was unique for Stoke, a totally new experience. Maybe that's another reason why I cried: because it felt like a bigger personal achievement in a way. We'd taken Stoke to a piece of history.

Tony came into the dressing room after the game and said, 'You know, you should all be proud of yourselves. It's a great achievement. We could've won it as well. Enjoy yourselves tonight and with family and loved ones.'

* * *

Then it sort of just began, slowly but surely, going wrong with Tony. It was almost as if we just drifted a bit. It was the same old training, the same old games and Stoke just ran out of gas under Tony. It seemed to be game after game that the ball hit out wide, into the corners; I was chasing it, putting it over for Peter Crouch to get a knock-down – and that was that.

It felt as if I had become a wing-back at times. I remember a game at Wigan. He really did play me at wing-back – that's never my position – and it was a nightmare. I did a couple of post-match interviews and I had a bit of a go in the media. I said that maybe if he played me in my proper position, I'd put in a good performance. I'm a winger, not a right-back or a defender. No chance. So I couldn't resist a little dig – and he wasn't happy!

He pulled me in and was screaming, 'If you've got something to say, then say it to my face!'

But it was true and I just couldn't help myself. The media are not stupid. They can see you're not happy. They watch the game and, if the performance has been bad, it doesn't take much for them to press my button and get me to say what I feel!

You don't really think of the consequences at the time – well, *I* don't! – and then it all comes out and goes wrong. Maybe your words get a bit twisted, the headline looks bad and all of a sudden my relationship with Tony Pulis was down the pan. Then it all blew up in training. And I'm thinking, 'Oh, fuck it! I'm going to have a fight with the manager!'

One day it just reached a point when another ball went

sailing over my head and I couldn't help it. I turned around and said, 'Fuck it! Why do we have to keep hitting it long?'

It drove me mad, having to ping long balls when we could have just gone inside, played football, played to feet rather than keep hitting it forty yards. I'm just here, for Christ sake! Pass it. Here I am! Honestly, it was mind-numbing after a while. If you want an insight into Tony Pulis's style of football then here it is. Long-ball rubbish, day after day after day. I finished by saying, 'Why am I even here?'

He just looked at me and turned and walked off and we continued doing our training session. It was that bad that he even stopped reacting when I was having a go at him!

After a while, you're going into games the way you're setting up, and it's just frustrating when you're out of the picture for twenty minutes because all he's doing is long ball after long ball. You're not in the game at all. It's as though the ball's flying over your head the whole time. It just got frustrating and annoying for me, anyway. Then, you know, in training it's the same old shit: shape, pattern of play, no fun whatsoever. Nothing was ever different.

So you go into training, go through the motions. I kept training, but I let my level drop because I was bored, and then he would complain that I was not making a proper effort. The problem was that we weren't training, we weren't working with the ball, trying to work on the technical side of the game, to improve as players or as a team.

I flipped again and told him, 'We aren't even training, we're not even touching a ball! You're telling us to run to number one, and we have to run over to number one, and if the ball goes near number two. . . We haven't even got the ball at our feet so what do you want me to do?'

I think we had one more row on the training ground after that. That was that season out of the window. Then he started playing people in front of me. Ryan Shotton, who'd played centre-back for Derby County. He was playing Ryan right midfield and I was thinking, 'He's taking the piss!' Fair play to Ryan. He was playing well, but he's a six-foot-three centre-back, not a midfielder!

So I had a moan about that and he came up to me and said, 'Look, you're doing well in training at the minute. Ryan's playing well. Keep going, keep going.' But at the back of my mind I was thinking, 'This guy, he's testing my patience here, ain't he? He's really trying it.' And you know, sometimes you just want to get results, and we'd be losing 1–0 or we'd lose 2–0 or 2–1 and I'd be thinking, 'For fuck's sake, we've got Kenwyne Jones, Peter Crouch,' two of the best headers in the Premier League at the time. 'Put me on the pitch, I'll find them – just play me!' Surely it doesn't matter if you think I'm a nutcase. I know that, when I'm on the pitch, I give 120 per cent. If I'm in training and I'm going through the motions, and I think the training sessions are absolutely boring, well, then, maybe I let myself down. But put me on that pitch and I'll always give it everything I have.

So, later on in the season, I wasn't playing; sometimes I wasn't even in the squad. As I said, when I don't play I'm a nightmare. I'll be the first to admit that. I would get so angry and talk it up.

Why am I not playing even when I'm trying my best in training (and I did sometimes, honest!) just to get back in the team? It doesn't change anything, so I tend to just throw it in.

* * *

I had the opportunity to go to Leeds on loan with Neil Warnock. I think I actually spoke to Warnock myself and he spoke to Sky. Warnock sold it to me, told me I'd be really good for Leeds. We got it all sorted with Leeds, agreed it with Stoke and the chief executive, Tony Scholes, and everything was done. Then Tony Pulis pulled the plug on it. He did it out of pure spite – 100 per cent. That left me absolutely buggered. Tony then claimed I was still in his plans, told Sky that I was in his thoughts and would be considered.

So I must be back in the limelight, then, back in the fold. But the next game came up Everton away – and he put me in the stand. I was absolutely raging. I didn't even go up to the stand, but watched the game in the players' lounge.

We lost 2–0. I walked into the dressing room. I had put

some bets on – not on Stoke, I hasten to add – and, as I was walking in, the team came back in from the pitch. They'd lost. I looked at my phone and my bets had come in.

So I shouted, 'Fucking hell – get in there!' I had made a fair few quid.

Then I looked round and one of Tony Pulis's assistants had seen it happen, looked disgusted and walked away. He obviously told Tony Pulis – and that's my luck. It could only happen to Jermaine Pennant! Should I have done it? No, of course not. Was I really pissed off? Yes. And that's why I did it. All I wanted to do was play football.

So, then, the next day was just an absolute car crash for me. Tony Pulis and his staff were cold. They were being funny with me, blanking me or giving me the cold shoulder. Fair enough, I suppose.

Next up was an away game. I think it was Manchester United or something.

The hotel was twenty minutes from my house and I knew I wasn't going to play. So I decided I wasn't going to stay there. I knew he was going to be a shit to me. He said, 'All report here seven o'clock for pre-match.' So I went home, got a good night's sleep and went to the hotel in the morning. When he came in, he pulled me aside and said, 'Where've you been?'

'Gaffer, I live literally twenty minutes away. Look, my little boy wasn't very well so I stayed at home.'

'Why didn't you call anyone?'

I said I didn't call because I didn't want him to say no.

MENTAL

So I took it upon myself about coming in. He said, 'Right, well, OK, fine. Get yourself home, then.'

He sent me home. So I wasn't on the bench, or in the squad, or in the stands. He just sent me home.

From then on it was just a nightmare. I walked into the training ground and he said, 'I don't want you fucking nowhere near this place when I'm here or my players are here. You can fuck right off!'

And I said to him, 'Look, mate, I don't want to be here; I don't want to be *near* you, to be honest.'

And he said, 'Good. Now fuck off!'

* * *

For a couple of months towards the end of the season, I didn't go in at all. I was still getting paid, but I was still getting fined because I wasn't going in.

I met the youth team coach and I said, 'Look, can I come in with you lot when the first team are not there?' He was OK with that and I just trained with the youth team as and when, but some weeks I was not in for training at all.

It's amazing how it didn't come out, but – fair play – they kept it in house. But, then, that was a bit weird because I was playing golf on Saturdays rather than playing soccer. So I'd go and meet some mates, have a round of golf and you'd get people looking. I could see them stare and say, 'What's Jermaine Pennant doing here? Stoke have got a game!'

I just kept my mouth shut, kept my head down and tried

to ride it out. Then one day I was due to play golf at a charity event. I was about to go out and Sky rang. He just said: 'Tony Pulis has left.' Fucking get in there! That was the best round of golf I've ever had in my life!

SKY ANDREW: It's difficult, because he had so much talent, worked hard at his game and yet he's found it hard to settle. He really should have stayed at Stoke, because he played well there, had some good times. The fans adored him and he played his best football at Stoke under Tony Pulis.

Stoke played a game, Pennant wasn't involved. Stoke lost and then Pulis got on the coach and there was Pennant laughing and joking. Pulis was saying, 'Right, that's it – I'm getting rid of him.'

At the time, I sided with Jermaine and was saying, 'Tony, what are you doing?' But, if you think about it, a manager doesn't want a player laughing and joking after a defeat. Pulis put him out in the cold. When Pulis left, Stoke gave him a reprieve. They said he could come back, two-year contract with an option to terminate the deal if he didn't come up to scratch. That was a major turning point for him, until Mark Hughes told him he could go.

His main problem is that he doesn't want to take responsibility for the way he conducts himself. You can't ever change until you take responsibility. You need to admit where you've messed up. He could have been a truly great player. He could have been up there with Beckham, ability-wise. His passing and his crossing are as good as anyone I've seen.

———

Some people wish managers good luck, give them a call or drop them a text. No chance! I was so happy Pulis had gone.

My time was running out at Stoke, but I actually really liked it there. I liked the fans, the club, the area. At the time my missus was from Stoke and she really wanted me to go back and play there. And I did, too.

So I said, 'Who's the next manager?' When Mark Hughes was appointed in the summer of 2013, I was a bit sceptical. He looks like a Tony Pulis-style manager with slightly better football. I was thinking this could be a problem.

But I was still buzzing from Pulis's leaving. And, to be fair, everyone at Stoke loved me because I did do well there in my prime. Tony Scholes, the chief executive, and I got on well. I was still at a good age. I'd been playing well before it all went wrong with Tony Pulis, and Sky then agreed a two-year contract. In the contract there can be a clause that we can terminate it if we want to, and they can terminate it if there've been any misdemeanours or whatever. So we agreed that. And then I met with Mark Hughes and we talked about what had happened with Tony Pulis. Clearly, it wasn't just his decision: it was more Tony Scholes and the hierarchy.

I got the impression that Mark Hughes wanted to be seen to be the one who was going to give it the OK, agree it and let me come back. Of course, he said yes because he wanted to keep the Stoke board on his side.

It felt good at first. I came on against West Ham early in the season, scored a free kick, scored the winner, and it was perfect. Start of the season it was, a couple of games in, so I thought, 'Perfect, I'm going to be involved now.' Then, for the next game, I was training hard and not even on the bench! And I thought, '*What?* I just scored you three points, mate. You having a laugh?' I was training well, working hard; there were no issues. And I still couldn't get a game.

For the following game at home to Manchester City, I was back on the bench, but I didn't come on. And it continued to be like that. It got to a point where I was thinking, 'Not again! For Fuck's sake, not again. *Why?*' He was putting me in the squad one minute, not the next, and I couldn't get my head round it.

But when things came to a head at Stoke, they came to a head suddenly. The real story of me leaving Stoke in 2014 – the reason why Mark Hughes, the manager at the time, decided it was time for me – was Bin Laden. It was New Year's Eve and we had a game on New Year's Day. We live in a private gated community – there's three houses and we can literally see the other houses from our front window. You just look out and you can see our neighbour's front door. They were having a fancy dress party for New Year's Eve. I knew I couldn't do anything, but I wanted to go round there, come home for midnight because even if I stayed at home I'd be up until midnight and I might as well go there and then come home. I wasn't drinking, the missus was going, taking the little one as well and I thought it would all be cool.

I went as Bin Laden. I had the plastic bullets around my neck, the AK bullets like I was Rambo and an AK-47 in one hand, a plastic one obviously, and a set of explosives in the other. I've gone there, and had a photo next to my wife Alice who was dressed as a dictator.

She then put it on her Instagram, and maybe Bin Laden was a bit fresh in people's minds! I had the full mask, the full white outfit and was dressed up to the nines.

That came out and then Stoke didn't really say anything. But I remember at the time that Sky was talking to a team in America. That story came out and suddenly the American team said: 'No, we're OK, actually…'

I think that story gave Mark Hughes the opportunity to get rid of me. I don't think he really wanted me. The reason I went back was because the board loved me. Tony Scholes wanted me, but Mark Hughes was new manager and if it was up to him, it would have been a no. He had to toe the line but, with that happening, it gave him the excuse he was looking for to get rid of me.

It was a shame, because I really did go home at midnight. I went home stone cold sober, but I should have got pissed because I got punished for it anyway!

Mark Hughes pulled me into his office, said they had

an option to re-sign me in January and that they wouldn't be taking it up. I was shocked, phoned Sky straight away and then Mark Hughes told me that Eddie Niedzwiecki had the papers for me to sign. To this day, I've never signed them! So, in a way, I don't know if I'm still a Stoke player now or not...Perhaps I'm still on their books!

It was a weird one with Mark Hughes because he could be very cold, very standoffish, and I think some of his staff are snakes. They say one thing to your face and another behind your back. They obviously had favouritism. It was all a bit shit, really.

It's just frustrating when you're training, playing five-a-side every week, not in the squad, not playing. They kept saying to me, 'You're good, you're in our plans, you're this, you're that.' And then you're training on a separate field with the stiffs, the players who are not on the starting XI. Then after a game the players do a warm-down, and the players who didn't play, the subs and the ones who weren't in the squad do a little five-a-side, and you're going through the motions again. Just making a token gesture. And it's all a bit shit because it was like that every weekend.

Obviously, Mark Hughes thought I was just tossing off, but I was just frustrated that I was not playing. I think that shows that I *want* to play. It's not as if I were just there picking up a wage packet. I was never someone who didn't care about the football or someone who just wanted the money. I *want* to play and it's when I'm not playing that the trouble starts. I love football, I love playing, and it hurts me when I'm not. I was never someone who turned up, trained and went home thinking about the wage packet. I trained and worked to play. And, when I didn't get the chance, that's when it hurts. I love to be putting in crosses. I want to be scoring goals. I want to be assisting. I want to be involved in that, even if I'm on the bench and coming on.

It was a sad end to my time at Stoke City, because I had a good time there with the FA Cup final. I connected with the fans and, Tony Pulis aside, I really enjoyed my football. I played some of my best football there, and I've got a few regrets, especially the way it finished. But some great memories, too.

CHAPTER 10

WOMEN

I've been out with some beautiful women down the years. That's what happens when you're a footballer. It tends to go with the territory.

There have been some ups and downs, good times and bad. I've behaved badly, been caught out a few times and been really naughty.

But there's one story that my mates still go on about now. If you asked any of my close friends to tell a story about me, they'd probably say, 'Ask him about the dog and the cats.'

I've never said a word in public before, because I know that the girl I was seeing at the time, one of my ex-girlfriends, Jennifer Metcalfe, would be absolutely devastated. In fact, if she ever reads this, she'll never forgive me.

We'd been going out for a while and, eventually, she moved in with me. The only problem was that I had a dog and she had two cats. There was always going to be a problem. Mine was a Japanese dog, an Akita, called Shadow. He had a white body with a black face. He was a very scary guy!

She had two white cats, really expensive Persians, special house cats. So every time they were in the house, we had to make sure the dog was outside. Shadow was a real beast and every time he saw the cats near the window, he would come racing up, jump at the door, try to get in – and he was an absolute menace.

Anyway, whenever we went away for the weekend, my mate Sam would come round to the house and check on them, make sure they were all OK. One day, we were away and I got a phone call from Sam. He was very nervous, really worried, on the other end of the line, saying, 'Are you on your own or with Jennifer?' I just told him to tell me what he'd rung for – he sounded in a bit of a state.

He said, 'Shadow's killed the cat. I mean, J, he's absolutely massacred it. That back door in the living room onto the patio, it wasn't locked, and he must've forced the door open. They must've been strolling round the living room. The dog must have thought, "I've had enough of this – I'm going to get them." One of them must have darted out of the door, the other one gone upstairs. Shadow must have caught one of the cats on the landing and there's blood everywhere.'

Sam took a picture of the scene on his phone and sent it to me. As he'd said, there was blood everywhere – like you've never seen. All over the carpets, the wall, on the banister. This Persian cat was very dead. I can't imagine the fear of the poor thing. It was a really horrendous, distressing scene.

I was feeling sick and panicking like mad. Myself and Sam came up with this story that the window in the wardrobe room had been left open and the cat had escaped through there. We had to organise a professional carpet cleaner to come round and a painter and decorator, because we needed to completely repaint the walls and get new wallpaper. They were a write-off – it was the full works.

I had to tell Jennifer that we could not go home straight away. Sam had to get the mess cleared up before we could think about going home. It was an absolute nightmare. Then, luckily, the other cat turned up, pining at the door, and we then took our time coming home.

I had to ask Sam had to bury the dead cat far away and very deep, because dogs sometimes dig up other animals. Can you imagine Shadow bringing in the dead cat?

And then, when we got back home, Jennifer was really upset for ages. She went around all the neighbourhood, saying, 'Have you seen this cat?' Then, at work, she printed off posters with a picture of the cat, offering a reward and putting up her phone number.

I knew all along what had happened, but I just had to play along with it. 'Oh, yeah, that's a good idea.'

There I was, driving into training, and I was seeing posters all round Liverpool appealing for a white cat. I was thinking,

MENTAL

'Shall I tell her?' But, until now, I've not said a word, except to my close friends. She even put a picture of the cat up on Instagram and I was thinking, 'Oh, God! If only you knew!' It was the most mortifying experience of my life.

So, look Jennifer, if you're reading this, then I'm really, truly sorry, but if I'd told you then we'd have broken up. . .

JON FORTUNE: He has been engaged on so many occasions, given out friendship rings and engagement rings so many times – he's done it each time to get himself out of trouble.

When he went to meet Rafa Benítez before signing for Liverpool, Rafa sat him down and said, 'What is stopping you becoming a top player? Go away, think about it and write it down.' He went away, thought and just put down, 'Chicks!'

He would say everything revolved around girls, going out too much because he wanted to be with girls, getting drunk on nights out with girls, and even the drink-driving thing was because he'd phoned a girl and she'd asked him to come round!

Down the years, I've got myself into various scrapes and situations. Undoubtedly, it's affected my career for the worse. And, if I had one piece of advice for a young player, it would be: stay away from women!

I think I'd probably been following in my dad's footsteps, having seen him with different women. You don't know different. You think your dad is always your idol.

When I first went out in London, at seventeen, I started getting a taste for it. Then I became better known because I was at Arsenal and was seen around the clubs.

Suddenly I would get a flock of birds, loads of girls. It went on from there. And suddenly you want to go out every week, pulling different birds, doing God knows what until all hours of the morning.

The more famous you become the worse it gets, and that's when all eyes are on you. Obviously, at first you just want to go out, have a few drinks, but the next thing you know you're in the papers for falling out of some nightclub.

I was always more into women than booze. I don't really like getting so blind drunk that I can't stand up. I hate the hangovers and feeling like shit. Why do you want to feel like that? It wasn't about getting drunk. It's fantastic going about with your mates, having a few beers and a laugh. But it was more about the birds, and, when you've got that Dutch courage in your system, you feel like the king of the world, and it's a challenge to pull a girl. Then you pull one and you want another, and another. . .

You get drunk, you talk to every bird, pull one, take her home, and next day at training you tell the lads all about it. They ask questions and you're telling them, 'She was filth, she did this, she loved it.'

The more you are in the limelight and the more you play

in the Premier League, the easier it is, and your standards go higher as well. Basically, you and your mates will go out to a club, you get your own table, some bottles of beer brought over. Then there will be this flock of birds a few steps away. They don't at first interact with you, but you're aware that they are there. Then there's another group over the other side. Then, before you know it, there are ten girls near your table. As the lads get more and more drinks in their system, the beer goggles come on and next thing you know you're calling them over and saying, 'Want a drink?' That's what they want. They don't want to be digging in their purses and buying their own drinks at the bar: they'd rather sit with footballers and get free drinks all night. They're coming over to get drunk and have some fun. They know about you, they know your profile. They're thinking, 'It'd be nice to bag a footballer.' What they don't yet know is that you are literally going to take them home or to a hotel, have sex, do all sorts, and probably won't speak to them again. We don't care, and the reality is that we just want a shag.

We used to call it Monopoly. You have all your 'properties' on the board, all different standards. For instance, you've got Mayfair (top quality) and Old Kent Road (the lower standard – no one wants to be there). So we would gauge each girl as a property on the Monopoly board. If she was fit and famous then she's high property, worth a lot, possibly Bond Street or Mayfair. Then there was a girl a lot of the lads had been with and she would be Old Kent Road. You get the gist.

I remember one of the lads coming up to me and saying, 'Here's fourteen quid.' I started laughing and just went, 'Old Kent Road!' It worked like this. If I slept with any girl and then any of the other lads slept with her afterwards, they would have to pay me 'rent': if she was Mayfair, they would have to pay me £100; for Old Kent Road it would be £14. Then, out of the blue, one of the lads would say to me, 'J, you owe me some money.' I'd ask why and they'd say, 'Lucy – you owe me £20.'

Most of the lads were involved, we are all embarrassed about it now but there was so much attention from girls that we got carried away. It was a game that went on for years – I suppose it just shows that we all had too much money and too much opportunity with girls.

I've had a couple of kiss-and-tells, but there are about twenty that Sky was able to stop. If you look in the *Mirror*'s or *Sun*'s archives, then I'm sure you'll see some in there. I've definitely had a kiss-and-tell done on me and there are some out there who just set out to trap you. If you're married, got a girlfriend or got children, it's more appealing to the papers as a story. They get even more money. To them it's like a winning lottery ticket.

SKY ANDREW: Because he was always in trouble, people thought they could write anything about him. One paper wrote a story saying that he'd had a fight outside a nightclub in Magaluf. He'd said something to a girl and a boxer had been there, hit him and knocked him out.

Jermaine rang me up. He was shouting, 'I'm not in Magaluf! I'm in bloody Greece.' His problem was that he told me so many stories that no one believed him when he told the truth.

For a lot of the girls, it's about hooking up with a footballer, luxury holidays, fast cars, nice homes and clothes, handbags. Who wouldn't like that? We all like being spoiled. You get your genuine ones. But the majority just want to be with a footballer, become one of the so-called WAGs (wives and girlfriends) and get that lifestyle, especially with all the reality shows now that just encourage them.

There've been so many stories about women in my life. I can't believe now that I was sent knickers in jail! That made my day for a bit, though. And they were clean – thank God! But that shows you that, no matter what a footballer has done, the girls still love to be around players and be associated with them.

On a night out, they make themselves approachable. If they come up to you they get embarrassed and make themselves look like bait, so they do it in a clever way. They float about, get some eye contact, and then, with some drink in your system, it's all systems go.

Everywhere I go, I see women staring. Be it in the

supermarket near my house, in the car park, wherever. But it would never work for them in a supermarket because, if I'm not out having a drink, I'm not interested. I was out with the lads to nick birds. People probably think I'm an alcoholic or just drink too much, but it's nothing to do with the booze. I don't sit at home and have a beer. There's never any alcohol in my house. It was just about getting leathered with the lads and then trying to pick up a bird.

It is as if it's guaranteed. If I want to, then I can go out and come back having done something with a girl. That would happen, without a shadow of a doubt. But, if you have a missus, a wife, then you have to keep it friendly, hold back and have some banter.

There've been a few times when I've tried to step out of my league. I tried it on with Baby Spice – or Emma Bunton, to give her her real name. It was in a nightclub called Pop. There was a VIP room in there, a club within a club. I saw her and I thought, 'That's Baby Spice – she looks all right in real life!' I think a Justin Timberlake song was playing at the time. I started dancing behind her, grinding away and I'm thinking, 'I'm in here. This would be a great one to tell the lads.' So I went to the bar, got a pen and paper, wrote my name down and whispered a few things in her ear: 'How you doing? You're so beautiful.' The usual old stuff. Then I slipped her the note, sliding it into her hand. She took it and then, at the end of the night, she went her way, I went my way and I never heard from her again. But she was with Jade Jones from the band Damage. Been with him for years. I didn't care. I flew in and thought it would be a good achievement.

I was always playing the field. It was just nuts. The number of times Ashley Cole and I had threesomes! He lived in Canary Wharf and I forget the girl's name now, but we brought her back and she was just up for it. We were high-fiving each other over her back. He'd be getting a blow job, I'd be at the other end. We had a little tea break and then went at it again. They just don't care.

We used to sneak girls back into hotels. To be fair, I think I've done that while I've been with every club. The thing with Arsenal and Liverpool was that you got your own hotel room. You'd just get on your phone and text them: 'Come round.' You'd leave the door open so there'd be no noise of knocking, and the next thing you'd know would be that they'd turn up in your room.

I'd say the majority of footballers still do that. For sure. I wouldn't say all of them. But there are a lot. If you've got a night game, you'd definitely get a bird round the night before. It doesn't have to be at night, though: you can get one to come round after your tea – have a bite at seven or seven-thity and then get a bird round at nine. And away you go.

It used to be a challenge to me that I'd do a bit with someone who worked at the club. When I was at Liverpool, I was speaking to one of the girls in the office. At Birmingham, I did a bit with one of the secretaries there. At Stoke, the standard was a bit dead, so I didn't bother, didn't even entertain it. At Arsenal, Ash and I got two of the ladies who did the TV and PR for the club. I had one girl in my room, and he had another at his apartment. I loved the chase.

I went out with the glamour model Amii Grove. I was engaged to her, although she's married to Chris Herd now, who played for Aston Villa. When we went out, I got caught cheating at times. She said, 'You always do the same thing – you always cheat on me. I want you to prove you're serious and propose to me.' Was that an ultimatum? She said yes. I was thinking, 'I'd only be engaged, wouldn't mean we're getting married!' I just asked in my living room if she'd marry me. It made her happy that we were back together. I gave her a big engagement ring and then she caught me cheating again and that was the nail in the coffin. She auctioned it off on eBay!

There was another girl called Anara Atanes. She was a crazy girl. She's gone through a lot of footballers, but I was one of the first back then. Her last boyfriend was Samir Nasri. I was dating her at Liverpool. I guess word goes round among footballers and we call each other to see who is seeing who. It becomes like a little soap opera, it certainly did with Anara Atanes, because I was getting calls from a lot of players to ask if we were together as she was supposedly going out with them. I got a call from Jermaine Jenas asking whether we'd been together. I said that we'd been together for three or four months. She was saying she hadn't slept with me. I said, 'Listen to me, I've been with her, I'll give you her number right now.' Then I told Jermaine which hotel she was in and even which room she was in. Then all of a sudden, she was denying it to Darren Bent! She had just messaged me to ask me not to tell Darren, so it wouldn't ruin things between them. But, if my friend asks me if I've been with a girl, then I won't lie. Then she was effing and blinding, calling me all the names under the sun.

Anyway, when I was dating her, I was seeing Amii Grove still. I was going back and forth. Anara used to live in Brighton and she messaged me, saying she wanted to come up and see me. I said I was up North. Then she said she'd come and see me, anyway. I was telling her not to. Then Amii came up to Liverpool, dropped off her bags and she and I went to the cinema.

When I got out of the cinema, I saw that my friend Sam had called me, saying Anara had rung, asking for directions and saying she was on the M6, whilst asking, 'Which turn-off is it?'

I couldn't believe it! I've got big gates at my house. Anara got to the premises, but Amii and I had gone for something to eat, thinking she'd give up and go away. But she climbed over the gates, let herself in (because I'd left the back door unlocked, as I'd got dogs), then remotely opened the gates and went back outside, drove her car in and chilled out in the house. Then she was messaging me: 'Where are you?' I said I wasn't staying there and I was away. But she was saying, 'I know you're staying here because there's a girl's bag here.' I was thinking that I couldn't go home. I had to tell Amii, and then we had to check into a hotel. I just turned off my phone.

Amii stayed the night at the house and the next day she was ready to drive all the way back home. I opened the gate and drove us up my driveway. Except something was wrong – I could see all of Amii's stuff floating in the pond! Anara had obviously gotten the hump, taken Amii's bag and thrown it, together with all its contents – clothes, make-up, the lot – into the water to chill with the carp. Inside, I was cracking up laughing. But I just said, 'I'm really sorry, I can't believe it.'

All the major stories have concerned Amii Grove. But there's another one where I had just signed for Liverpool. An Irish girl came up from London. She was leaving on the Sunday and then Amii was due to arrive on the Sunday night. I'd timed it all perfectly. This girl stayed for one night, I dropped her off at the train station and then went to pick up Amii. As I did so, I thought, 'Perfect timing.' Then I drove Amii back to the house and pulled in, and the girl I had dropped off was standing there outside. I was thinking, 'Oh, my God!'

The weather was so bad with snow that her train had been cancelled and she got a cab back to my place. And here was I, dating Amii. I looked at the girl and then thought, 'What do I do?' They were looking at each other, obviously thinking, 'Who's that?' I opened the door, walked in, went upstairs and they both walked in as well. They both then came upstairs. I didn't know what to do. Amii was saying, 'Jermaine, what's going on?' To be fair, the other girl backed me up by saying nothing had happened, that her train got cancelled and now she was here. Amii was asking her if anything had happened but I couldn't hack it and went downstairs because I was shitting myself! Then I'm thinking, 'Imagine if they both stayed and we all did a bit!'

I was thinking of every scenario. I gave her £400 to get a taxi from Liverpool to London. Amii was livid and it took her two days to believe me and get over it. I just can't help myself.

There was one girl I had to pay £16,000 after we had a one-night stand. She rang me and told me she was pregnant and that she was keeping it. I asked her, 'Excuse me – how do I know if you're pregnant? I don't even know your surname!' I was outraged. I have no idea if she was telling the truth or not but it ended up with me paying her £16,000, her going on holiday and deciding to not have the baby.I've heard that happens a lot, girls telling footballers that they're pregnant and you either pay them off or have to deal with all the hassle. I didn't tell anyone, not even my agent or closest friends. It's fair to say that some girls saw me as an easy touch.

* * *

I met my wife Alice in the gym, where we had a cool-down day. It was on a Monday. We'd both been working out. She came out of a class and that's where I saw her. She had to walk right past me while I was on the treadmill. I was thinking, 'Mmm. . .' I spoke to some of my mates who lived in Stoke and they told me who she was. I said to Ryan Shotton, who always went out in Stoke, that, if he saw her, he should give her my number. He actually saw her the next week and he came back and I asked, 'Did you get *her* number?' Ryan said, 'If you want it, you'll have to get it yourself.' How was I going to do that? I went on Facebook or some other social-media site and sent her a message saying, 'Ryan said that I've got to ask you myself. So here I am asking for myself.'

A week went by and I didn't hear anything. Then she messaged me to say hi and told me she was coming back from London on the train – and it went from there. That was in 2011. She was very attractive, a nice girl to conquer. We just got along, and here we are now, seven years down the line and married.

That's the only time I've been married – and it will be the last as well! She's been great, really supportive of everything. I'm not an angel, as we all know. But she's always been there for me.

My career has been up and down. We have to move wherever my footballing takes me. But she's got a daughter as well, so she wasn't able to move to Singapore with me. She's still digging deep, taking care of the house, looking after stuff, and she's the backbone of our marriage. Now I'm older, wiser and growing up. Trying to prolong my career, behaving well.

CHAPTER 11

LIES, LIES AND MORE LIES

After I left Stoke in 2014, I found it incredibly difficult to get a club. I was in good shape, a free agent, and was getting lots of interest.

Quite often I would be going into clubs. It would go really well. I'd do some training, be about to sign – then the door would be slammed in my face.

Sky Andrew had his suspicions that someone must be putting down the poison, because it seemed that every time I was about to sign, it came out in the press, people knew about it – and then, bang! A club that had wanted to sign me suddenly changed its mind. It was impossible to understand.

That was when I realised that someone *had* been putting down the poison for me at clubs, telling them that I had surgery on my ankle, I had a hernia problem, I wouldn't pass a medical. He doesn't do this, he's not paying that. They were coming up with all sorts of rubbish. His wife's this, he's out all the time, and all sorts. Now, if you're a businessman or chief executive and you get an email like that, then you're probably thinking, 'Fucking hell! We don't want this. He's bad news.'

I remember Sky saying to me at the time that he thought someone was sabotaging me and making it difficult for me to find a club. I was getting frustrated with him, taking it out on him. I think I got released in January and I didn't sign up again with anyone until November. I was doing my nut. It was absolutely crazy.

This person tried to ruin my career. They contacted Tony Scholes, the chief executive at Stoke, and also rang up Tony Pulis. Pulis is a family man. I always wondered why I struggled so hard after I left Stoke. Even to get in the door to train with a club was hard. It was nearly always no-go. Towards the end, I always wondered why things went so bad. I know that they phoned Tony Pulis and told him that my life was a mess. I was always going out, didn't care about anything, didn't look after myself. After that, I just couldn't get a club. Sky would ring clubs and they wouldn't let me even train. We began to wonder what had happened.

Fair play to Sky – it was him who was first onto this sabotage act on my career. I was at Charlton, doing some training and working really hard, and the manager was saying he was impressed with my attitude and wanted to sign me. Then two weeks went by and the manager pulled me in and said that they hadn't got the budget, that they'd have to sell some players first, and yet I knew it was bullshit because they were going to buy a player from Wolves for £250,000, so they clearly had some money.

Sky is close with someone at Charlton and he found out that they received an anonymous email – we know now who it was from. It said, 'Do not sign Jermaine Pennant – he drinks, I know he takes drugs.' And everything you could think of they were saying. We asked Charlton for the email. They told us off the record, and yet, when I signed in Singapore, the chairman pulled me and said he'd received an email and was concerned. He didn't want anything going on. I said, 'What email?' He'd got an email from someone with the same name as my son, laying out all this nonsense about my wife, my lifestyle and everything.

But it didn't work. They signed me. So they contacted the press in Singapore and were trying to tell them stories about me. But my new chairman in Singapore stood up for me, threatened to sue the papers and so instead they approached me for some quotes.

I told them that it was all lies and that people were trying to destroy my career.

I have been reckless in the past and sometimes you only truly appreciate something when it's gone. That's what it felt like at times with football – that someone was maliciously trying to take away my lifeblood, and at times I felt powerless to stop it.

MENTAL

In the midst of all this, the depression it was casting upon me came to a head during a night out I had a few years ago, in predictable fashion and with predictable results – another drink-driving conviction. I had arranged for my wife Alice to come to a game, and left her tickets on the door beforehand. After the game, I went up to the players' lounge, but she wasn't there. I soon discovered why. I went home and Alice had moved all of her stuff out of the house. She'd moved out because of more lies that had been picked up and spread right across the internet. They were untrue and just spiteful.

So, in a fit of gloom, I messaged my mates and they got me out for a few beers to try to drown my sorrows. I went out, told a mate to get me a hotel and he booked it and got me a room key, and we'd arranged to meet at a club. But I rose to some bait, got into a heated argument, and got taken outside to cool off by the bouncers. My head had gone and I just thought, 'Fuck it – I'll drive home.' So I drove home, got stopped and pulled over and was done for drink-driving again. I know it's no real excuse, but that drink-driving episode was the result of being at the end of my tether.

It has taken me a long time to learn, and spot trouble. Of course, I know that it's still no real excuse to drink and drive. But when you feel as if someone's trying to ruin you, wind you up, split up your marriage and then poison your career, you can do stupid things, things you regret. It's not a symptom of being a lost cause, or a broken human.

Sometimes life just gets its foot on your throat and you react badly.

It's been hard throughout my career, making my own mistakes, seeing bad headlines about things I've done wrong. But, then, for a figure from my past with an axe to grind to make up lies and stories, invent injuries and allegations with the sole intention of trying to ruin me is something I can never accept, nor forgive.

It also nearly drove a wedge between me and my wife Alice, putting lies about us. That is just open warfare.

Hopefully, my life is now in a better place. I'm more settled and, despite everything, this person has not been able to ruin me.

That was a real low point for me but, finally, I can begin to understand what was going on and, now people know a little more about me through this book, maybe they can make a better judgement about me as a player and a person – and about my life.

CHAPTER 12

KIDNAP PLOTS
AND
PORN STARS

I've done some crazy things in my time with cars and holidays. I've had some wild times.

But two of the maddest episodes came while I was on holiday. And I'll admit that I've set some pretty high standards for myself down the years with some stupid things.

Like the time, just days after playing in the Champions League final in 2007, I passed out drunk on an EasyJet flight from Spain. I don't do things by halves. I don't do the normal things that a footballer does and, generally, I do what I do in the full glare of the media and get myself in all sorts of trouble with embarrassing headlines.

I'll come back to that holiday in Spain, but a couple of holidays that they didn't find out about – or at least I don't think so – concerned a kidnap plot and being arrested in Mexico.

As mad as it sounds, I was petrified. I feared for my life when I was warned that I was at the centre of a kidnap plot. Yes, someone actually plotted to kidnap me, hold me to ransom and try to get some money for my release.

Down the years, I'm sure there've been a few people who would say they'd never pay it, no matter what they were asking. But I was genuinely worried that I was about to be taken away and tortured! Honestly, it felt as if the world was closing in as more and more people seemed to know about it.

It all happened on a Greek island, Zante. A girl came up to one of my mates and said, 'Listen, there's these guys who are thinking about kidnapping Jermaine.' She was saying that they'd contacted the papers asking how much they would get if they sent photos with me all beaten up. I said, '*What?*' The girl was deadly serious.

There were a few of us out there, on holiday, and we'd been told about a boat party, and had all been invited. But this girl was telling us not to go because she'd been tipped off that that was where they were planning to kidnap me. She seemed to have inside information, because she knew everything about what was going on. Not only that, but, while we were getting a drink at the bar, some meatheads said, 'I wonder how much we'll get for you, then.'

It sounds really weird when I recall that Jeff Brazier was there with us, and he got a call from back in England talking about it. We thought nothing of it at the time and just laughed it off. But, when the girl said she, too, had heard them asking how much they'd get for pictures of me kidnapped or beaten up, it quickly became a bit more serious. I was saying, 'Fucking hell!' It was our last night and I just said, 'I'm not getting kidnapped for anyone.' And so, on the final night of my holiday, I stayed in.

So I was in the hotel on my own, and suddenly the electricity cut out and all the lights went out. I was shitting myself. There I was in the pitch black, stuck at the hotel – and waiting for someone to come bundle me into a van!

It was like a movie and I was waiting for the cops to burst in! All the lads were out on a party boat, having a whale of a time, and I had stayed in by myself to be safe. And so, of course, the lights had to go out, didn't they? You'd better believe I was shitting myself.

The guys who had been threatening me at the bar – and were maybe behind it – were muscle-bound, clearly on steroids and pumped up to their nut. There was no messing with them. So my strategy was to just lock myself in my bedroom in the dark. I was as scared as I've ever been! On this occasion, thankfully, it must have been dodgy Greek wiring rather than a taskforce breaking in, as I remained un-kidnapped until morning.

JON FORTUNE: He was on holiday with Paolo Vernazza and we all went out there and met up. It was on Zante in 2005. It wasn't a great place. We chose to go there rather than Ayia Napa. It wasn't our cup of tea but we enjoyed it, anyway. He'd just got out of prison, gave this little speech, and Jeff Brazier was there as well. There was a boat party. Someone warned us off that, and Jeff got a call from back home about a newspaper running a story about a gang asking around about what it would be worth for them kidnap him and get photos of his face slashed up.

Then, a girl warned us off about rumours that there was a gang on the island planning to kidnap Jermaine. We had to keep him out from there but, believe me, he even found it difficult not to go out that night even though it could have been really dangerous – even though he could have been kidnapped.

We used to have some wild holidays – Cancún, Marbella, Ibiza. We would go absolutely nuts. It would be fantastic.

But one year it got a bit out of hand and I was arrested in Mexico! We were just rowdy in the street and, honestly, it wasn't our fault. Someone threw a plastic water bottle; it hit Jon Fortune in the head. Some Americans, locals and tourists were there.

I know Jon shouldn't have done this – while he thinks he *should* have done it – but he went over and hit one kid. There was a real commotion. My mate Paolo Vernazza was absolutely wasted. He was so drunk that he couldn't really hold it all together.

There was a bit of shouting, a bit of argy-bargy, and, next thing you know, the police have turned up. And, let's be honest, Mexico isn't the sort of place where you want to be arrested!

We were just standing there when the police came, and Paolo was all over the place. For some reason, the police had gone to Paolo – maybe they could see the state he was in – and arrested him. The police got his hands behind his back, handcuffed him and threw him up against the bonnet of a car. I said, 'Whoa – what's going on?' They just grabbed me, did the same to me. I was trying to help Paolo out and ended up getting arrested. I was thinking, 'I've seen these films – and they're ruthless.' They took us to the station and put us in a cell. Paolo has got a neck chain on. They made us take everything off, the chain, shoes, everything. Because Paolo was drunk, it was not registering properly. They were telling him to take off everything, demanding his chain. But Paolo was saying, 'You're not having my chain.' He was too drunk to understand the situation we were in. They were saying to him, 'Take it off or we'll take you into this room.' But he refused. They took him into a room and all I could hear was: '*Aargh, aargh!*' He was in pain. When he came out of the room his chain was missing. He had been saying he'd never hand over his chain, then they'd given him some digs and he'd handed it straight over.

MENTAL

I wanted to piss myself with laughter. They locked us up, put us in different cells, and I could hear him singing Akon's single, 'Locked Up': *'Let me out. . .'* There I was, arrested in Mexico, in a police cell, and I was crying with laughter!

Thankfully, the lads had followed us to the police station and had enough money to bail us out. We had to go back the next day to get Paolo's jewellery and my earrings and whatnot.

It was so funny – certainly a holiday to remember.

* * *

Another holiday that was amazing was the one I mentioned earlier, in Spain. It was just after the Champions League final. Then a few of us went to Marbella for four days and had a wild time. That's what I liked doing the best: going away with mates, having fun and just being a bit normal as well. I like to think not everyone has to be the same and that players can still have some fun and not give the same old story of behaving well, taking each game as it comes, blah, blah. You've got to have fun and I was determined to make the most of it!

We partied throughout our last day: pool party, nightclub. Then we went from the club to the hotel, packed our bags and went to the airport. We must have had nearly twenty-four hours' drinking. I was saying, 'Oh, my God!' I ordered some breakfast, couldn't really eat it, and just wanted to get home.

I was feeling like shit. Everyone was looking ragged. I was drinking as much water as I could and I wanted to detox. On the plane, I was sitting near the window. Thought I could have a decent sleep and then we'd be home. Plane takes off, five minutes, ten minutes go past, and I start feeling a bit sick. Was looking for the little bag and thinking, 'I'm going to be sick, I'm going to be sick.' The seatbelt signs are on and it's getting worse. I'm sweating and thinking, 'I need the toilet.'

The stewardess was telling me to get back to my seat. It was an EasyJet plane and it was packed. I was halfway down the aisle, saying, 'I'm going to be sick, going to be sick.' Next thing I knew I was waking up, on all fours like a dog, sweating my tits off in the middle of the aisle. The stewardess picked me up, put me at the front of the plane and gave me oxygen. So there I was, at the front of the plane, wearing an oxygen mask, breathing from a tank, and I had an ice pack on my wrist.

They were questioning Jon and said, 'What's he had? What drugs has he taken?' Jon was saying that we'd been on an all-dayer, had come straight to the airport with no sleep. I was almost in a coma. Apparently, there was talk that they would have to turn the plane around because I was so bad and they were worried I couldn't fly. I thought I'd got away with it as far as the press was concerned, gone undercover – but then, a couple of days later, it was in the papers! I'd got caught again.

I was quickly learning a tough lesson: I couldn't do

anything in public and get away with it. Especially the sort of stuff that I was getting up to.

So, I'd played in the Champions League final and – fast-forward forty-eight hours – there I was, passed out on an EasyJet flight. Most big players would go first class on a luxury jet, then to some luxury resort. But here was I, on a bog-standard plane, completely passed out, drunk after an all-day bender. That's just typical me!

I've had some crazy, wild times, done some stupid things. But I've got to admit that I've blown so much money on cars. The car that everyone remembers is the 'mirror car'. I got an Aston Martin DBS and wrapped the whole thing in chrome.

People would always say to me, 'You've got this amazing car – and then ruined it!' But I loved it. It was great to be different, do something crazy, and it was fun. You would certainly get noticed. I'd get pulled over all the time with my reputation – and that one made me a sitting duck!

It wasn't cheap on insurance – they never are – but I loved to treat myself, and cars were something that I could never resist.

My top two cars are a Ferrari F430, all black, and the DBS, the chrome one. They were great cars. They cost a fortune. The Ferrari cost £160,000 and the DBS was £120,000. When you sell them, you don't get all the money back. I bought the DBS for £120,000 and sold it for £70,000. That's some depreciation! But, if ever you want a nice car, try to get a used one off a footballer because we tend to change them all the time – and lose thousands.

Some players who buy cars have so much money that they practically give them away when they buy a new one. As soon as anything becomes trendy, you've got to have it. Such as a matt-black car or a car decked out in mirrors.

I've had some nice cars, but the worst I've had wasn't nice to drive. It was a Lamborghini Dorado. If you drive it on the road you can feel every pebble, let alone every bump.

I used to be into cars but I'm more of a family man, not so fussed now. A nice four-by-four will do me. I've had my fun, enjoyed the flashy lifestyle, and it's like any aspect of life in that you can grow tired of it. Some people might like watches – and I've had a few of those – but, as you get older, you can chill out a little bit.

These days I'm happier going on holiday to Dubai, chilling out with Alice, enjoying some relaxing time.

Honest, I really have calmed down a lot as my career has gone on – I needed to!

JON FORTUNE: He's had an incredible career, a great life, and he's a brilliant fun guy. He's great company and I know a lot of footballers but, believe me, no one has got as many stories, got themselves into so much bother and had so many near misses as Pennant!

He's a bit of a throwback, a lot of fun. A few years back, players probably used to have more fun but he's a real throwback to good nights out, parties and wild times.

I think Pennant gets on with English managers because he's like that throwback: a cheeky kid from the days when the old-school players would go to the pub after training.

I know people will say he could have done more. But he's had a great career, done far more than most players.

Liam Brady said recently that Jermaine's been a huge success; that what he's made of his career is incredible bearing in mind where he's come from.

And he's absolutely right.

I might be calmer now, but I know my tattoos catch the eye these days and maybe give a different impression of who I am now. Everyone looks at them. The trouble is, they become addictive – and I still want more.

I got my first tattoo when I was seventeen. It was a schoolboy error of a tattoo. But I was young. You make mistakes. It was a love heart of my first girlfriend, Lindsey Brown, at school. We were together for four years. It had her name in the middle of a heart with a ribbon. Now you cannot see that at all. It's been banished!

It's all gone now I've had so many. You get one on your shoulder; the other shoulder looks bare, so you get another on that one. One thing leads to another, and the next minute they're everywhere. It's been ongoing for about twelve or fifteen years. I'm all covered now. There's not much space left. Tattoos are addictive. Hopefully, I'll get a few more. . .

Although, they were the cause of one of the crazier things to happen to me in recent times: ending up on the front of *The Sun* being called a porn star. There I was pictured on the front page in February 2018.

What they said about me, being some kind of porn star, is a load of bullshit. Premier League Ace turns Porn Star – I mean, come on, what a joke. I couldn't believe I found myself on the front of a national newspaper for that. It's ruining my image, my reputation, I know it's not always been great, but it can have major repercussions.

The reality of what happened was that Alice was on her laptop, I came into the room, was just messing about, put my hand on her leg, I didn't actually do anything, you can't see my face, just my hand was on the shot. Someone has put two and two together, seen my tattoo, took a picture, and sold it to *The Sun* and they ran it as me and my wife putting on a sex show.

They came round to the house, buzzed on the gate and asked if we'd got anything to say. We promised to take legal action if they printed anything and the next day when the story ran the missus was fuming.

It's more for her daughter. Kids now can find anything on the internet – she's quite popular at school because of her mum and obviously me as well. She was more worried if the other kids would find out. Luckily enough no one did, so nothing was said.

To me, I've had it all, you get used to it. I was just thinking: 'It's tomorrow's chip paper.' But for the next day or so, Alice was so upset, wouldn't go out, she was distraught. I felt bad for her but I'm used to it.

We want to take action. It's been screengrabbed – if you go to a cinema and record a film, then you will get done. She never gave permission, never gave the paper permission, and they are in trouble for that and for calling me a porn star.

I remember when the story came out, she came running downstairs, absolutely in pieces, I was playing a computer game and she came in screaming: 'They're running the story, they're running the story!' She was so devastated, and this is what they can do, they don't care. They would ruin someone just to sell a paper. To make the front page is just ridiculous. I could understand if I had my willy out, taking part – but it's just my hand!

To see myself on the front page, I couldn't believe it. It made me think I'm still relevant – good news or bad news.

Look, she is a glamour model, we've been together for seven years and I've known that since day one. She's not seeing anyone, not meeting anyone, she doesn't work in a strip club and yet still probably earns more money than some Championship footballers! Er, let me sit back for a bit – hence why I've not always been playing!

People will have an image of her, but that's not here at

all, she's totally the opposite and it doesn't bother me. You go to Marbella, Vegas, Ibiza and girls will be walking topless on the beach so it's neither here or there.

But we're also in a relationship because of who we are. It works. If there was an issue then we wouldn't be married, for starters, and it wouldn't have lasted for this long.

The next couple of days after the story, we made a joke of it. No one really made out like it was a problem. If we went to the shops or walked down the street, I'd be thinking: 'Oh, I bet they're all thinking: there's the two porn stars!' It's a bit weird. But we're pretty normal, really!

CHAPTER 13

OUT EAST AND UP NORTH

Having played for two of the biggest clubs in the world, Arsenal and Liverpool, and had a great time at Stoke City, the final chapter of my career has also taken me to some interesting places.

I had the opportunity to play some football in the Indian Super League, played there for seven weeks. I went there for the experience. I played well and that finished in late December 2014.

Since then, I also went to Singapore to play with Tampines Rovers and I have to admit that I found that an incredibly frustrating time.

But, between India and Singapore, I also had a very happy time at Wigan Athletic when I played under Malky Mackay. He was great for me, absolutely fine. He's a really nice fella, straight up, no bullshit, and I like that. He's one

245

of the nicest, for sure. He tried to help me out after Wigan, recommended me to other clubs, and he was top-class. We got on really well and I'm really sad that it didn't work out for him.

I like Eric Black, too. He's a good guy and knows his football, a good coach, knows what he's talking about. You can talk to him, have a laugh with him. He's not too serious. Sometimes you feel a bit uneasy when you talk to people. You don't want to be seen as answering back when actually you're just offering an opinion and hopefully get good feedback from it.

MALKY MACKAY: I got a call saying he was available and he was on a free, because he was a free agent. We were desperate for players at Wigan at the time, especially players with a bit of experience. I did a little bit of research on him, phoned a couple of people who had worked with him and coached him as well. The general consensus wasn't bad at all.

I'm not one for preconceived ideas, so I asked him to come in. We gave him two weeks' training, and at that stage no one would even give him training facilities. We did the first session. He and I went for a walk and I asked him to tell me about himself. First thing I noticed was this smile on his face – he was a happy boy. He was as fit as a butcher's dog, not an ounce of fat on him, and you don't lose technical ability.

He told me he felt he'd been a Liverpool player and, after that, you think your career goes the other way. He'd tried eleven clubs. No one gave him a chance – that Jermaine Pennant, ex-Liverpool player. No one wanted to know. From that day on, he was absolutely fantastic. He just wanted a chance. He told me it wasn't about money. He just wanted to play and train at a good level.

He was a positive personality in the dressing room. He was bubbly. He was a personality on the training ground and you need that these days, because players can be a touch quieter. After that trial, it became clear there was no way on earth we were going to let him go! He was way too good and important for that. He was terrific – professional, committed, a terrific boy. He absolutely did his bit for us, scored a couple of fabulous goals. He wasn't always happy at not lasting the whole game but, again, that shows me that he wants to play.

He was happy to settle down, make a new life with his wife and family in a little village in the middle of nowhere in Stoke. Maybe the penny dropped for him later on in his career. I left Wigan and then he called me to ask whether, should anyone call for a reference, I could put a word in. I was really happy to do that. He was right up there with the best players I've worked with and coached.

Technically, he was top-class. I could see

that every day in training. He influenced games. I remember one game at Rotherham United. It was an important game for us, to keep us involved. He scored two free kicks, ten minutes apart, from the exact same position on the pitch. They were sublime, absolutely sublime. They were of a very high quality on a technical level. You could see he had played at a high level in terms of his vision, for example.

I had been to Millwall to train before I joined Wigan. That was a bit of a last resort, but Ian Holloway, the manager there at the time, was a top guy; he was brilliant. They were happy. They had booked a hotel for me to stay in while negotiating. Then, before I could go back there to do the deal, I got a call from Wigan inviting me in. It was a no-brainer, because it was less than fifty minutes from my house.

Wigan had just come down from the Premier League. It was a bigger club at the time, so I went in to train and I had to text the chief executive at Millwall to say I couldn't make it. Then it quickly came out that I was signing for Wigan. Andy Ambler, then the Millwall chief executive, came out publicly and said they'd booked a hotel, they'd paid for this, that and the other. It made me a hate figure. Then, sure enough, one of the first games I played for Wigan was against Millwall! The abuse I got was a joke! 'Where's our fucking money? Give us our money back!', the Millwallers were saying. It was at Millwall's ground, the Den, as well, so anyone who knows Millwall knows it's pretty bad at the best of times.

I did well at Wigan, particularly with free kicks. I scored with two against Rotherham and one against Fulham, and almost scored another against Bolton. I think I took five free kicks and scored three of them in the whole time I was there. I put something up on Instagram saying that Cristiano Ronaldo took eighty-four and scored twelve. I said I was not saying anything, but those were the stats. As you can imagine, I got some stick, but a few positive replies as well.

Sadly, Wigan went down, but we agreed a contract. The new chairman, David Sharpe, came in and we verbally agreed something. The club and the fans liked me; they were on board and they wanted to re-sign me. A couple of weeks later, they offered a contract. We rejected the first offer, then we negotiated and agreed something. But, a week later, they came back and said the new offer was off the table. I think the chief executive came down hard and didn't want to sign off the deal that we'd agreed with the chairman. I got annoyed. I rejected it. And yet, in hindsight, I think it would have been better if I had taken it. It's probably one of the things that I regret most.

If I'd taken it, I would have been in the Championship for two seasons, because it was a two-year contract. But I turned it down, believing I would get a better offer, which I did, from Rotherham. Then Sky was saying, 'Rotherham

– it's not the greatest place, is it? Where can you go from Rotherham?' Sky was saying there was no way back from Rotherham. He put me off. I do regret that one.

That was off the table, but then they came back with another offer, better money, a signing-on fee. And they came back three times and really wanted to sign me. I met their manager, Steve Evans. He wanted me and they kept coming back and eventually gave me an ultimatum: to sign by 6 p.m. or the deal was off. I was ready to take it.

Then Sky rang me and said he had some good news: he'd got a deal for me in Dubai. Massive dough. He said there was a 90 per cent chance that he could get me a contract. I had always wanted to go to Dubai and play there, so I just said, 'OK, let's do it.' I called up Rotherham and turned them down. Then we were trying to negotiate a move to Dubai, and then, suddenly, it didn't happen. You have to accept it as one of those things, but I went nuts at Sky because I had to take my frustration out on someone. What could I do now?

I went three or four months with nothing until Singapore came up. It was like a stepping stone. Asia was becoming big and, if I felt I was doing well in Asia, I thought it would give me a better chance to get somewhere at a good level in Asia. But the football in Singapore is not great at all. They get just 850 to 1,000 people at some games. There is zero atmosphere. The way the club is run is a complete shambles.

We had a big game in the AFC Cup, which is equivalent to the Europa League. We went to the airport – all the team were going. We were all in our own, ordinary clothes. I was thinking, 'Why?' We didn't think much of it. We all looked as if we were going on a stag do. But the reason was simple: it was cheaper and easier to get a tourist visa than to get a proper working visa. So we all turned up in our normal gear. I was there with my passport and there was a mix-up with my visa. I had played in India before, had a visa when playing in Mumbai, and they got the wrong date and wrong visa. I was thinking, 'We've got an important game in two days.'

So I had to go home. They flew off and there I was, back in Singapore. Then I had to come back with a new visa, fly back at 8 p.m., meet someone, get on the plane and then land at 11 p.m. Then we'd got a game in two days. It wasn't good preparation. It was a shambles. That's why I wanted to come home. It's hard to adapt.

It's a totally different way of life, but I like something different and I'd enjoyed the Spain adventure. But the problem with Singapore was the lack of atmosphere. It's hard to motivate yourself with no atmosphere. No matter how professional you are, if you've got one man and his dog, then it's very difficult.

The people were very nice when I arrived, couldn't do enough for me, but it didn't end well. I was disappointed. They said a few things and that was a shame.

But I gave everything – and one man doesn't make a team.

* * *

MENTAL

We came second, didn't get anyone in the Team of the Year, yet the team that came sixth got four players in that competition. The team that won everything got only one! Something is not quite right with the way the football is organised there. It's outrageous.

We had a few national players, so we were expected to win everything. But the difference between the national team and the local players is hardly anything there. We were far from being a superstar team. They looked after me and were great at first, but, as soon results didn't go our way, it all turned a bit. At the end of the day, I can't stop other teams from scoring! One player can help a team but he can't do everything. It takes more than having just one star – this isn't the NBA.

The standard was not great. I wasn't sorry to leave. I came out for the experience and to try something new. But it didn't really work out.

* * *

I'd like to see out my career in England, and finish in a good place. These days I call home just outside of Stoke. Just outside of Shropshire. That's my base and where I live.

That's why, when I came back from Singapore, I wanted to play for a club up North after being abroad for so long. Even though it was a drop down to League One, I was very happy to sign for Bury in January 2017. My friend Paolo Vernazza knows Chris Brass, the manager at the time, and called him. I got invited in and went, saw what it was about. I spoke to the missus about it and she said it was perfect, just down the road, so we wouldn't have to move house, and it would be easy for me. There were no major offers and so I just thought, 'Why not?'

I didn't really want to play in League One, but it would keep me ticking over, get me playing again – and I liked it straightaway. There is a good atmosphere, good banter in the dressing room, a nice environment to be in – and it's fun.

There were good lads, a good dressing room, a good team. But playing in League One is hard. Teams around you kick it long, squeeze and it's hard. That's why some big teams lose in the FA Cup to lower teams. It's direct, and you don't get time on the ball. They're in your faces and they can really make it difficult. If we were up against teams who get it down and pass, then it was easier. But it's hard in this league.

I had other offers. I had one offer in Thailand, had a few offers here. I wanted to stay in this country first and foremost.

* * *

And so it was to Billericay Town, who were paying a lot more than clubs in the league.

I commute twice a week to go training, and I did actually think that it would be a lot easier than it is. I thought the players would have a higher IQ in terms of football knowledge. I've played for Arsenal and then Liverpool in the Champions League, so everyone thought this would be a walk in the park. I would look like Messi. But it's not like that. It's actually harder, because you have to do more.

I've become a bit of a marked man and if I don't score or assist goals, then people think I've not done my job. But what the coaches don't understand – no disrespect to Glenn Tamplin, the owner and manager, but he's not done any coaching badges and doesn't always get it – is the number of times I assisted a goal by making a decision with the right pass, at the right time, and making the right choice. If you look at Sergio Busquets at Barcelona, you'll see that he doesn't make loads of assists, but he makes it tick, makes the right pass and never gives it away.

That's what I try to do: make the right pass at the right time for things to work. The Billericay team told me that they didn't think I was worth what they were paying me. I said, 'You what?' I had a conversation with some of the boys and they were saying that was nonsense. I never give the ball away, I kept it, made things happen.

Non-league is more long-ball and I've never been a player to score ten and twenty goals in a season – I've always been someone providing assists.

The owner is a businessman. He likes the publicity. The more he gets, the more he attracts in terms of attention and investment, and I get that. But it wasn't to be here.

The day after my ridiculous 'porn star' story broke in the press, Billericay put it out that they had let me go as if it was because of the story, but it wasn't like that. It had been going on a while. Glenn Tamplin, was talking as if I hadn't done enough, not given enough. Then I was talking to some of the boys, and I was thinking: 'Bullshit.' His assistant told him that I faded out of games, was good for fifteen minutes and would then go quiet for fifteen minutes. I had to explain and say: 'Listen, Glenn, this is non-league, players in non-league will drift in and out. If I'm not getting the ball for fifteen minutes because they're hoofing it up the pitch, or if the right-back is not passing to me, what do you expect me to do?' If I was playing central midfield then fair enough, but being on the wing is different and because he has no formal football background, I genuinely don't think he understands and he expected me to score, assist, do something in every game, I kept explaining that just because I wasn't scoring or assisting, it doesn't mean I wasn't having an impact. I could be involved by making the pass for the goal, or create something going forward. A football man would understand what I did on the pitch, but he couldn't see that.

He's like a fan coming to take charge of the team – he couldn't see what impact I had on the team if I didn't score or assist a goal, and I began to realise that there was nothing I could do or say.

Also, because we were doing so well, he was thinking that he didn't need me, Paul Konchesky, Jamie O'Hara and could let us go. It started to get a bit bitter, but I stayed humble, agreed to get a pay-off and leave the club.

Then he called me back a week later to offer me another

chance. 'Another chance – are you having a laugh?' I'm fine, thanks! Then we stuck to the arrangement and we parted and went our different ways. Since I left, they've really struggled.

The bitter thing was that after the porn story broke, they announced the day after that I'd left, put it out on Twitter and so on as if that story had something to do with it. It's totally unfair, as I had left a month earlier. Alice tweeted back and said: 'He left four weeks ago, he wanted to get away from the circus and needed to get away from the shenanigans going on.'

It is a circus. Glenn Tamplin is a bit bullish, doesn't know how to manage the team.

Billericay did become a big story. It was a media feeding frenzy, there was a documentary and TV show on it, the players got a bit distracted when they should have been concentrated on the football.

We lost our first game of the season and then went on an incredible run and suddenly he's expecting us to win every game three or four nil. Then, if we didn't score enough, he'd say he was trying to sign a striker when actually we had a top scorer who was very good.

Glenn is a difficult character, emotionally up and down. If you had a contract with him, it's as good as toilet paper. It's worthless. When you're at a proper club, you sign a contract and you know your future is secure, what the future is, your family is safe and at Billericay it can change from week to week.

One of the players, Ricky Modeste, got an international call-up for Grenada. At non-league level, that's incredible, but Glenn wanted to fine him for reporting up. He wanted to fine him! You can't do that, it's in the FIFA rules.

Then he got another call-up, went away and yet Glenn told him that if he didn't play he'd get fined. So he landed at 7.30 a.m. and played for us at 3.00 p.m. He was just up and down – but that shows you the lengths he will go to.

I can't see they'll ever get into the league as the club is now. It's sad. Initially, it was really good. I thought we could do something good, I felt it was a good project to be involved in.

The travelling was a bit of a ballache, I went down twice a week for training, and it was three hours one way from where I am near Stoke. It was OK in the beginning, but then you get a bit bored of it.

But I would always turn up. Then you also get fed up with it all – we were top, winning every week, scoring most goals and conceding the least. But because he had spent so much money, Glenn expected us to beat teams every week by 4–0, 5–0 and it was an all ego boost. It wasn't about the team, it was about him.

I remember we drew a game, he came into the dressing room, punched a hole in the wall! We drew! We were top of the league, we'd lost one game all season.

Then he's losing the plot and screaming: 'You could have tried harder, you've let me down.' We're top of the league.

MENTAL

Then his assistant, who is right up his arse, is chiming in: 'He's not got where he is today without giving everything.' They just don't seem to understand that football isn't just about trying hard and working hard. It takes a bit more than that. If that's all it was, then teams would have cracked it by now.

Glenn loved the attention. He is a dream for the press, and as soon as it fails then it will all come crashing down. He's not making it easy on himself with all the attention he brings upon himself. It also affects the players – you never see managers carrying on like that in the professional level.

It's the craziest club I've been involved in. By far! I've never seen scenes like it anywhere else. I know it's non-league, but it's off the scale compared to any other club.

Glenn did some crazy things. It was always a soap opera, always a circus. We had one game against Harrow or someone and one of the players, Sanchez Watt, told him that he couldn't make training because he had a photo shoot. It was his day job, he did some modelling. After all, it was semi-pro and work commitments can come into it. He'd actually given him the dates, and then the time comes and he didn't turn up for training. Then the game and we're all getting changed. Then Glenn suddenly says: 'Sanchez – put your clothes back on, you're not playing. If you want to do your modelling then fine, but you're not playing.' He's let him get changed then he's tried to humiliate him.

There was another time when Glenn suddenly said:

'My son said to me: "Dad, why if the players score do you pay them a bonus, but if they don't score why don't they pay you?"'

Glenn brought it to the table, and said it was a very good point: 'If you cunts don't score – you should be paying me!' Talk about manmanagement skills!

CHAPTER 14

WHAT NEXT?

Since I left Billericay, I've become more settled in my life. I honestly don't go out much. I just chill out. It's a different way of life as you get older, but I'm still passionate about my football. That said, I'd be open to going abroad eventually – especially if I got £1 million a week to play in China! But we'll see what happens.

SKY ANDREW: I am going to have to look after him for the rest of his life. I'm going to have to find something for him, get involved in some sort of business. I don't mind doing that, because he was the problem child who overachieved because of what was going on in the background. He really has overachieved, when you consider everything. I was best man at his wedding and in his speech he said, 'Come on, Sky, pull another rabbit out of the hat for me.' That's how he saw me; that's what he believed; and he always thought I'd produce another rabbit out of the hat. In a way, I don't actually know if I helped him. He created so much chaos wherever he went and yet I still helped him. He was sent to prison. I got him a move to Birmingham. He was on a lot of money there and had just come out of prison. At Birmingham, he was drinking, turned up for training drunk and played with a tag.

At Liverpool, he was great for a year-and-a-half. Then he messed up again. I got him a move to Real Zaragoza. Then at Zaragoza, he told them all sorts of stories. Once, he told them a story that he was going to London to see his dad because he wasn't well. But, instead, he went to Marbella and there were pictures of him partying there in the papers. He always thought he was smarter than everyone.

Post-career? I'd like to get into coaching, definitely. I've not done my badges. I was due to go to Wales or Ireland for a week and do them a couple of years ago, with a few of the lads from Wigan, but I couldn't make it for one reason or another. I'd like to do it, though.

I definitely feel I've got something to offer coaching-wise. Every good player can offer something, I like to think.

We'll see if and when the time comes and see what's the best option for me.

I look at someone like Kevin Nolan and he's doing really well. He's still in touch with the players, young enough to have a connection. If you're that bit older, then you might fall out with them, the training might be boring and you have no connection with what's going on in the dressing room. If you're that bit younger, you can relate to the players. There are a lot of young managers in the game now – even the old-school managers now have a tendency to bring in a younger coach. Eventually, I'd like to become a manager, for sure. I think I'd connect well with the players and, if they did well, then I'd give them a few nights off – don't worry about that!

If I don't get into coaching, then I'd like a move into TV. Everyone says I'd be good on TV. I like to think I've got a sense of humour and people tell me I've got a bit of character, bit of banter and can be funny. I've done some TV stuff in Singapore. I really enjoyed it. I can remember a lot from my career, can offer some insight, and it's all fresh.

I think sometimes players can be retired too long, be pundits, and yet be out of touch with what goes on now in some dressing rooms or at clubs.

But I can give opinions on what the teams are like, what a league is all about, formations, tactics, how hard it is. I don't have to do too much background work because it's all fresh and recent in my mind, so I know it already.

MENTAL

Coaching, for instance, is quite interesting. I don't think there are too many good crossers of the ball in the game at the moment. You have to work on that whip, really study your crossing. I used to stay for a long time after training to work on my technique. It was more about shooting, trying to place it in the top corners and really getting used to kicking the ball in a totally different way.

It's about practice and perfecting the technique, especially on free kicks and dead-ball situations. So I think my coaching would definitely be on the attacking part of the game.

You do get goalkeeper coaches. You get general coaches. They teach you the basic, the main areas, but I think there's room for more attacking coaches. They might start throwing that in by the time I finish.

* * *

And now a word about racism. I think I've been lucky in that the only time I've really encountered racism in football was when I was playing in the Champions League for Liverpool in Turkey, against Beşiktaş. I went to take a corner, and I could hear monkey chants. Euro coins were being thrown at me, lighters thrown at my head. I went across and thought, 'I'm not taking this. It's a danger zone over there.' Everyone was looking across and saying, 'What are you doing? Just take the corner.' They didn't realise, until I started pointing at the crowd, what was happening. Then I started ducking, covering my head. Then the ref came over and blew his whistle, and some of the players tried to calm it down. Jesus Christ! That's the only time I've experienced it, but it was scary as shit because they wanted to kill me.

I've never really seen or been through any of that kind of stuff. I've been lucky to have played at clubs with good fans and also in a good era. It did come back for a little while, but I never really felt it.

I remember one time while I was with England under-twenty-ones that we ended up having a whites-versus-blacks game. The players didn't care and I could see the coaches were looking on and saying, 'You can't do that!'

But all of us, the players, were saying, 'Come on, then – let's do it!' It was the players who suggested it. We were picking teams. Everyone was picking his mates and the next minute it was becoming black versus white. The white team was professional. They had Peter Clarke. John Terry, Gareth Barry and a few more. Then we had myself, Jermain Defoe, Joleon Lescott, Shola Ameobi and Shaun Wright-Phillips. Absolutely no discipline. We got battered, because all we wanted to do was score goals. It was light-hearted and it was funny. I think it was Peter Taylor who was the manager, but it's something that never got repeated!

I actually had some good times with the England under-twenty-ones, as well as some stupid stuff, working with some really top players and having a good laugh.

There was this thing called 'Eggyboff'. It's a game we all

played. Someone would say, 'Eggyboff – the first person to move.' As soon as you move, you become Eggyboff and no one will talk to you or acknowledge you in any way – until someone else becomes Eggyboff. You become the invisible man. Cruel and unusual. It's a bit like 'Simon Says' (do you remember that?). Someone suggests something – usually a bit daft – and the others follow.

The first time we did 'Eggyboff' was when David Platt was in charge of the England under-twenty-ones. He took training, five-a-side games, and he liked to join in because he thought he still had a bit. I don't know who shouted it out – probably I did – but the call went up: 'Right, in training, Eggyboff: you can only use your wrong foot.' If you were right-footed, you could use only your left and vice versa. You saw people in front of goal, about to shoot, change their mind, run around the ball and kick it with their weak foot. It was so funny. People were going to ridiculous lengths to use their weak foot. Everybody was doing it. My left foot is normally just for standing on. It was like swinging a golf club when I was kicking with it!

Honestly, it was one of the worst training sessions that I've ever been part of. No one could kick it properly and we were falling about laughing! Then, after training, David Platt said, 'Right, boys, that was a great session!' We just looked at each other in complete amazement. 'Gaffer, if you only knew!' It was all about the banter.

Another incident was in the Championships themselves with the under-twenty-ones. The first game was against

Italy. We went to the stadium a couple of days before to get a feel for it. We were driven there on the team coach, had a look round and then walked round the pitch. The idea was to be very serious, take in what it was like, experience the ground and so on.

We were mucking about, winding up the substitutes, or 'stiffs', as we called them. We sat on the bench. A few of the stiffs sat down and even they were laughing, knowing that they weren't playing. 'This is where I'll be sitting, keeping my seat warm.' It was a good atmosphere, a few laughs, good banter. Then someone shouted, 'Eggyboff – the first one to move.' The whole squad were sitting on the bench. The coaches had walked off, the security had walked off, everyone had gone and they looked back and shouted, 'Come on, boys, we're leaving now!' We were there for forty-five minutes!

They had to bring in the security with the dogs to try to get us to move! You do not want to be the first to move. In our case, because it was the whole team, they couldn't really do anything. By the time we eventually got on the bus, they were absolutely livid. That game still goes on now.

Then another one was under Les Reed. On the way to training, we pulled up at the training ground. The coach told us to get off the bus. The nerdy boys got off and, of the rest of us – Gareth Barry, Jlloyd Samuel, Shaun Wright-Phillips, Joleon Lescott, Jermain Defoe – someone said, 'Eggyboff – first one to move.' The rest of us were going, 'Take it back, take it back!' No one could move. We were all stuck on the coach. It was half an hour! Les Reed had to come on the coach and give out the bibs.

We had this joke going on and no one could break it. It was so hilarious. Then Les Reed was shouting, 'You lot think it's fucking funny!' But it wasn't just one of us, it was everyone, and there was nothing really they could do. Defoe and I were right at the back, hiding. We could see Les Reed handing out the bibs. You could see his glasses steaming up, ready to have a fight!

It was a good laugh around the under-twenty-ones and there were some really good players. But, just as at club level, more players should really come through.

When I was at Arsenal, we had a great youth team. Won the FA Youth Cup. I was there, along with Ashley Cole, Paolo Vernazza, a lot of good players. With the talent we had, so many more should have made it. It was just that era that not enough kids broke through. Look at the players we had. Top players. But there were fantastic players blocking their path at Arsenal. The only one really to break through was Cole.

But, apart from that, no one really made it. It's the same old story now and the discussion about players and youngsters coming through. It's so difficult. I don't know if Arsène wasn't really that keen on bringing through young players, particularly home-grown ones. I don't know if his attitude changed or the league's rules have changed it for them, but they definitely bring more through now. But if we'd had the same players now as back then, they wouldn't have broken through. There just weren't the openings for the youngsters then. Simple as that.

I don't know whether the team was superior back then or whether Wenger had a different mindset and was reluctant to bring players through and became more open to it. But something has changed in his thinking because the players of today wouldn't have broken in back then. No way. Maybe they've learned from not opening up a pathway to give young players a chance.

Ashley Cole could have joined Crystal Palace permanently. He went on loan and, if they'd had the money, he would have signed for them. But the reason he got the chance was that Sylvinho was injured and they threw Ash in as a last-minute thing. I remember watching the game and he did well. He didn't look out of place. And then Arsène threw him in the next game and the next minute he'd been moved up to the first team, got moved into the changing rooms with the rest of them and became a regular. But it was only due to Sylvinho being out that he got his chance. If he didn't get that chance or Palace had the money, then he might not have got the chance to become the player he was for Arsenal, Chelsea and England. It's amazing how close it can be.

Would he have got the same platform or chances had he gone to Palace permanently? I doubt it. And that just shows that sometimes it's not about players making it if they are good enough. They also need the chance as well. Just look at Tottenham, who're giving young players a chance under Mauricio Pochettino.

MENTAL

Ashley was of an age when he wanted to play regular football and you need a touch of good luck as well.

The problem is that we definitely need more players to come through for the good of the England team because, sadly, there's no doubt that the current squad are not great at the moment. The best squad had Beckham, Gerrard and Lampard. The Golden Generation under Sven-Göran Eriksson reached the quarter finals and now England seems to just drift off.

As a league, English football is fantastic because of the Premier League. But as a national team, England just haven't performed, really.

In every tournament they just seem to underperform and it's just crazy.

CHAPTER 15

MENTAL?

I reached a point in my life when I seemed to be spiralling out of control. I was always making certain decisions that would end with my doing the wrong things for myself, my relationships and my career. I was always pressing the self-destruct button. I knew I was doing it, but I wanted to know *why* I was doing it.

It was caught up with Alice, my wife. Why was I cheating the whole time? It was affecting my football; it was affecting everything. It probably started because I got caught out cheating again and ended when my wife and I almost called it a day.

From that point, I wanted to go and see someone. I wanted to know why I made all those decisions, why I would end up pushing people away whenever they got close, why I hurt people who *did* get close. I couldn't understand it. I knew I loved my wife, I know I still love her, and I couldn't understand it.

I went to see a psychologist when I was in England, and she pared my situation down to the bare bones, took it right back to where it started. We went back to my childhood. This is why I can remember so much, why my recollections have been so clear for this book. It's because I have re-examined it all, right up until the present.

The psychologist could see that when people do get close, I just push them away. I'm not used to having a maternal figure or a mother on the scene. I've not had that in my life. When people get close, I get worried that they are just going to leave. So I make certain mistakes, bad decisions, and try to justify someone getting close, looking for excuses to get attention from elsewhere.

It was more to do with my wife and our relationship and why do I make bad decisions regarding us, and from that it affects football as well. The decisions I was making would affect my playing career.

From the first incident of my drink-driving, everything I do wrong, including drink-driving, is to do with my girls. There came a point where it felt as if I would be left with nothing and with no one in my life if I continued down that road. You might think I'm blaming everyone but myself, but there has to be a reason, a root cause, as to why things go wrong.

That's why I really wanted to go and see someone to explain all my misdemeanours, all my womanising; I wanted to know why I was cheating so much. I seem to have done something wrong to every girl I've ever known, ever been with.

The psychologist wanted me to explain it, wanted to break it down from the bare bones. She said I crave the attention, that it fills that gap from when I was younger. She said that if I get bored or get lonely, I will crave that female attention because I never had that, never a mum whom I could call up. The bond with a mother figure sets you up for the rest of your life and you learn how to treat women, you learn how to behave, and yet I never had that bond with my mum.

I have the same problem now. I crave attention from women to fill that gap, to make me feel better. We spoke about that and we looked for the underlying reasons as to why, the reasons for my mistakes, and why I'd built up a lot of stuff that I'd never told anyone – everything from growing up to what I've been through and what I've seen. That was good to get off my chest and get out in the open. She helped me move on and see there was light at the end of the tunnel to help me get on a better path, follow a better direction.

I had about six sessions with the psychologist. At the time, it was obvious that I needed help because something was going wrong. I was hurting my wife almost every day and she basically said that I either get help or we call it a day. She couldn't understand the things I did to hurt our relationship. I was caught out cheating again and, while I can see it's not normal, I was almost doing it as if it were complexly normal and it was something that I did on a regular basis, as if I didn't care.

It was then that I realised help was needed. We reached a point when we realised that, even if it didn't save our relationship, then the problems would keep on happening and would end up ruining my life.

I couldn't understand why I needed to do all the things I was doing. Then, when the psychologist broke it down, it did tend to make more sense. It gets better and better and now we have a trust between my wife and me and things are where they should be.

But one thing's for sure: I will always tell young players to stay away from women!

Of course, I have to look back and take responsibility for my actions. The drink-driving is my biggest single regret, especially the second one. I was at Arsenal. I was still young. Sky Andrew had been to Arsenal. My contract was coming to an end, and he'd gone in and tried to get a new one. David Dein met with Sky and agreed it. David said to Sky that I deserved it. They offered me £20,000 a week and in that era, for my age, it was an incredible deal. But I didn't know this. I didn't know that Sky had met up with them, had spoken with them and agreed £20,000 a week.

It was a week later that I crashed the car and got caught for drink-driving. After that, another week later, I went on loan to Birmingham and then signed for them. If I'd stayed in that fateful night, I might have remained at Arsenal, won trophies, still been in the Premier League. Who knows?

The worst thing about that was that I actually went out, got back at about three or four in the morning. I actually felt fine. I was indoors at the time. Then I got a message from a girl. She was in a hotel. Did I want to go round? At that age, I was as horny as anything. As we've seen, I'd been drinking, but I told her I was coming and that I'd phone her when I was there. I felt fine driving. Then I jumped in the car, hit the kerb and then the lamppost. I was speeding. There was a little hill you have to go up and down, then it turns right. I was following the satnav, making sure I was going the right way. I got over the hill, looked at the satnav. The road bent. I looked back up quickly and thought, 'Shit!' Then I hit the road and the lamppost. The police came and breathalysed me. I messaged the girl and said, 'I don't think I'll be coming!'

The first time was doing a U-turn, I was just over the limit. I got done the second time when I was a week away from completing my first ban and then Sky had also agreed a £20,000-a-week deal with Arsenal.

But the truth is that I've got only myself to blame. I know that. It's partly my upbringing, but I'm also old enough to make my own choices.

From seeing how my dad used to live, I think the womanising is definitely in the genes. Seeing him move from one woman's house to another woman's house. Hearing little stories from his friends as I grew up about how he behaved and stuff. Your childhood all plays a part in your adult life. Everyone who doesn't think it does is fooling themselves or lying because it puts an imprint in your brain, often in your subconscious, that you might not be aware of.

You feel it's normal or acceptable. It's in your genes and it feels as if you are beyond help. All those issues play a part as well.

But I think that accepting that, understanding that, has really helped me and also my marriage.

The reason why I didn't open up to my wife before was that I felt embarrassed. I struggle to be open and honest with anyone. I never show emotion. Having grown up on my own, and from always being on my own, it's the way I've dealt with everything, and I've put a block on it. That's just me. Having no one to turn to as a child meant that in my adult life I've not shown any emotion. I've shut everyone out. Of course, it was emotional seeing the psychologist, but it also felt good because it was a weight off my shoulders as well. It made me open up more to my wife about issues, tell her how I was feeling. I could open up about things, when I didn't like something, when I felt down, when I was trying to keep it in.

It has definitely improved our relationship. It made me grow up as well, realise what's important. I don't need to mess around the whole time. Until this point in my life, it's been like an addiction. I crave it. People get addicted to drugs and drink. My addiction was getting that attention. I needed it to fill that gap, whatever I was craving. As soon as someone – particularly a woman – showed interest, I was happy.

My problem was that I didn't have many people who were close to me. I didn't have friends I would speak to all the time, people I could confide in, and certainly not a mother figure I could talk to. With me, my friends could often be distant. I would go through periods where I wouldn't speak to them for two or three months, and yet, when we spoke on the phone, it would be as though we had spoken yesterday.

With women, I needed the attention the whole time. My wife wasn't enough. I needed to speak to other girls as well. She was understanding. She was the one telling me that I had issues, it was the last straw for us, and I needed to see if it could help us.

We were going to try relationship counselling. But it wasn't her who was the issue; it wasn't her making the mistakes. She said to me that it was I who needed to see someone. I needed to sort myself out.

It's definitely brought me and my wife closer together. There are so many people out there who try to sabotage things for us. We've reached a stage now where she's trusting me again and slowly we're rebuilding that trust. Now I don't need to worry so much. I don't pick up my phone every two minutes and text a girl.

While attention-seeking may have been down to my upbringing, at the time you don't know why you're making crazy decisions. You think it's normal. You look upon yourself as just a guy having fun, playing the field and having a wild time. You never think it will reach a stage where it will ruin your life.

MENTAL

And, of course, that's when it reaches the point at which you have got to help – you absolutely *have* to get help.

There came a point when I made decisions to go out on a Friday night because of a girl. I would break curfews and club rules because I wanted to see a young woman. But I had a game the next day. I wasn't just hurting people around me: I was damaging my life and my career.

Even in those early days. Remember that hat-trick I scored for Arsenal in the biggest game of my career? And I'd been out the night before and got wasted. Just because the boys were going out. I thought: 'It's an *FHM* party. There'll be girls there!' My first thought should have been, 'It's my first start tomorrow; this could be my big chance, so I'd better stay in.'

Most footballers would have stayed in. But that's just not me. It was all to do with girls. It's not as if it were about drinking. Yes, it's got me into trouble, but I don't like drinking. I don't even like the taste. You get a hangover and it gets worse and worse as you get older. That's what people think. They think all my problems are to do with drinking and that it's booze and going out partying that is the biggest problem.

But it's really not. It's nothing to do with drink. I go out for girls, not for the alcohol. I never, ever sit at home and have a beer. There's never any alcohol in my house. While I've been in Singapore, I've virtually stayed in for two months and you'd never catch me staying at home and having a drink, because there's no booze in the house. I've never had a drinking problem. People have no idea. All I do is go to nightclubs or bars, try to pick up girls. Then, of course, you're going to have a drink with everyone else. Then you get a confidence boost. Then you can get everyone you want, get the beer goggles on, and it's a free-for-all.

It was useful just to get to the bottom of my ability to press the self-destruct and see why everything kept gong wrong for me. Things could be going so smoothly with my wife, then, all of a sudden, we'd have an argument, split up, get back together, and then it'd be fine for a while. Then she would do something to piss me off and then I'd get the hump, go out, talk to a girl, and give her my number, start talking and flirting.

Then I'd be on Instagram. I'd 'like' a picture, start sending messages, get her number, and it was like a little pattern. It would always be the same. That's why I saw someone professional to talk to about why I did this, and it was very helpful: it helped me to get through difficult times and realise *why* I needed attention from women. You must understand that most of the time I wouldn't actually sleep with them. I would just be messaging them, speaking to them and flirting with them, messing about because I wanted the attention. I just needed that. I craved that attention, to know that someone else liked me or was interested in me. To feel as if I were the centre of attention. Rather than speak to my wife if I had a problem, I would go and message someone, message another girl, to make me feel better.

That wasn't normal. Everyone has problems with their relationships. Six months into a relationship everything seems perfect; there may be a bit of Barney Rubble, but no real arguments. But rather than talk face to face, I would bottle it up, not say anything. I would keep it all in, then look for someone to help me feed that addiction, that craving for attention from another woman.

I do think I'm a lot calmer as a person as a result of that understanding. Yes, I'll make more mistakes. But I feel happier about myself and my relationships. All that was brought home to me in very real fashion in March 2018, when my grandmother Cynthia died. She was so important to me, she was everything to me growing up, she was like my mother. She literally was. I fell out with most of my family at times, still do, and yet all the while she remained neutral, she told me not to worry, I was always her little grandson. Whenever anything that happened to me, she'd be worrying about me. When I went to prison, she told me she couldn't eat or sleep through worry. The same with any story or scandal: it would affect her like I was her own son.

She was such a caring woman. She would tell me off all the time, give me a piece of her mind; she told it how it was, she wouldn't hold back, and that was good for me.

I didn't see her as much as I should have, which I regret now, but when I did see her, her face would light up and it meant so much to me.

But we gave her such a great send-off in Nottingham, she would have loved it. There were people outside the church, because so many people turned up that not everyone could get in. She was so well known and liked in Nottingham.

My dad gave a speech, and I said some words to thank her for being the best grandma ever – and also being a mum to me. I just said I wished I could have done more. I shed some tears and my dad came up to console me a little bit.

She had an open coffin and everyone paid their respects; I gave her a kiss on the forehead. It was a very sad time, but the grave was beautiful and it was a very nice send-off, knowing that she's now in a better place.

It just goes to show that even with arguments, petty things, you need to cherish what you have because you never know what can happen. You should cherish your family.

I was so happy that before she died she got to come to the wedding and would come to some games. I remember she came to the wedding and, before the party began, she went to leave, so I asked her where she was going. 'I'm going to get changed, put on my party dress on and have a party!' She went back to the hotel, put on some younger clothes, came back and had a right old dance. 'Grandma – you're not twenty-five anymore!' But she loved a dance. I'm glad she was there, witnessed a happy day for me and enjoyed it.

I remember she came to one game at Liverpool and, like I said, she didn't hold back. I introduced her to Crouchie, Peter Crouch. There was not even a 'Hello' from her – she got right to the point. He walked up, said hello and introduced himself. She stood there, looked him up and down and just said in her way: 'Boy, you're tall-eee!' She'd just say what was on her mind. God bless her.

MENTAL

***

My career? People always ask me about my career and the first question is: should I have done more? The truth is that I'm very happy with my career and what I've achieved. But I know 100 per cent that I could have made more of myself and my ability, definitely made more of my career. I know I could have been playing longer in the Premier League; my whole career could have been in the Premier League and been at the top the whole of the time. If I had taken the right path, lived well and behaved better, then I would have been right up there with some of the best players without doubt. I know 100 per cent that I would have played for England – 100 per cent. Maybe if those drink-driving incidents hadn't come into play, also, I would have played for England.

Everyone gets a cap these days. I do think I have a natural talent and, if I'd pushed myself a bit more, maximised my potential and also got to the root of my problems a bit earlier, maybe it would have happened for me.

But my dream was to play for Liverpool. I've done that. I've had a great life, great times, amazing fun and, hopefully, this book will help people understand me a bit better.

Once people get to know me, I like to think they can see I'm mischievous. I like a laugh and good fun, but maybe they will come to know that my heart has always been in the right place.